D0899107

BY SABRINA ORAH MARK

Happily
The Babies
Tsim Tsum
Wild Milk

HAPPILY

HAPPILY

A PERSONAL HISTORY, WITH FAIRY TALES

Sabrina Orah Mark

RANDOM HOUSE • NEW YORK

CARLSBAD CITY LIBRARY
CARLSBAD CA 92011

Copyright © 2023 by Sabrina Orah Mark

All rights reserved.

Published in the United States by Random House, an imprint
and division of Penguin Random House LLC, New York.

RANDOM HOUSE and the HOUSE colophon are
registered trademarks of Penguin Random House LLC.

Most of the essays in this collection were originally published
in slightly different form in *The Paris Review.*

Hardback ISBN 978-0-593-24247-6
Ebook ISBN 978-0-593-24248-3

Printed in the United States of America on acid-free paper

randomhousebooks.com

1st Printing

First Edition

APR 1 3 2023

To Noah Juniper and Eli Winter,
my moon and my sun

The future has an ancient heart.
—CARLO LEVI

Contents

Prologue

As a child growing up in Brooklyn, I had a book of fairy tales I never opened because on the cover it had a salivating crocodile in a brown corduroy vest who I imagined would eat me if given the chance. "There was no such book," says my mother. "You're imagining things."

The cover was flecked with gold, and its spine smelled faintly like fish. I search for it online. I type in "fairy tales, crocodile, brown vest, salivating." I type in "1985." I type in "I was afraid." "It looks like," says the computer, "there aren't many great matches for your search. Try using words that might appear on the page you are looking for."

What I couldn't open as a child, I want to open now. I am ready to read all the fairy tales in a book my mother insists never existed. Fairy tales about witches with long knotted tongues or children baked into bread or daughters who run so far away from home they grow a second heart. But I can't find the book.

"Are you certain," asks my husband, "it was a crocodile and not an alligator? Are you certain the corduroy vest was brown?"

But my husband isn't really looking for the book. It's for me to look for and for me to never find. There is a path of pebbles inside that book I will never follow. There is an unlived life that begins eleven pebbles in. I am so far away from where I've never gone and what I'll never know and who I'll never be, it is impossible to tell if on that path I am radiant or falling to pieces.

"What are you thinking?" asks my husband.

"Nothing," I say. I pick a crumb from his beard, put it in my mouth, and swallow.

Home is so far away from home.

My husband is painting the steps leading up to the front of our house. I chose the color, Echo Blue, and after he's finished painting, I stand across the street and look at the steps and the brightness of the blue confuses which way is up and which way is down. I choose a darker blue. Cosmic Dust. And then I choose an even darker one, Overcast. And then a lighter one, Blue Promise. My husband mixes two blues together and then adds white. There is something wrong with all these blues leading up to my house. While he repaints for the fourth or seventh time, a mole gets stuck to the curled edge of the painter's tape at the bottom step. With the patience of a man who for three days painted and repainted the same six steps, he tenderly peels the tape from the mole's velvet leg. For a split-second, the mole stays dead still, then struck by freedom tunnels back into the soil.

I rarely even use the front stairs. I mostly enter from the side.

We settle on a blue called Haze, which I think is really the shade of all the blues mixed together. I decorate the sides with broken Mexican tiles and seal it with grout.

A neighbor comes over to take a photo. "Oooh! It's like we're in Morocco," she says cheerfully. But we're not in Morocco. We're in Athens, Georgia.

How did I end up here? And why have I never left? How does anyone end up anywhere?

My mother calls. I tell her about the Mexican tiles and the blue stairs. "Take a photo," she says, "and send it to me."

"You wouldn't like it," I say. "It's very colorful."

"You're probably right," she says. "I hate colors. What's that noise?"

"It's a bird chirping."

"Well," she says, "it's way too loud."

My mother and I are six states apart. Not counting the states we're in.

Thirty-five years ago I was a Yeshiva kid rocking back and forth in a gray wool dress praying with all my might to a god as mysterious as the fairy tales I never read. My backpack was heavy with the *siddur, chumash,* and *mishnah* I carried from my mother's house to my father's house and back again. I wore a shell of scripture. I wore a path. And now I am in Georgia raising two Black Jewish boys and wondering if we should get chickens.

"Chickens?" says my mother. "For what?"

"For eggs," I say.

"That makes no sense," says my mother.

Before my parents split, their hatred for each other created a hole in our house my brothers and I tunneled through searching for a path that could bring us home. In fairy tales, there are paths made of needles and pins and crumbs and pebbles and yellow bricks and beanstalks and golden tresses and the notes of a magic flute and girls running for their lives. The thread a girl pulls through a lost boy's foot to sew his shadow back on is a path, too.

Fairy tales themselves are well-trodden paths. I scratch at its dirt with a stick. Letters appear like a scattering of seeds. They spell my name. They spell your name, too. Even if we've never been here before, we've been here before. I scratch at the dirt again. A small white pebble—no, a baby tooth that could easily be mine or yours—appears. We thought we lost it as children, but it's been here the whole entire time.

"If not for you," says my son Eli, "I'd be nowhere."

"If not for you," I say, "I'd be nowhere, too."

A large tree branch falls from our neighbor's tree, damages his fence, and lands across our driveway. This, too, is a path. This sentence is a path. And this book is a path. Like stretches of ancient roads, I connect pieces of fairy tales to walk me through motherhood, and marriage, and America, and weather, and loneliness, and failure, and inheritance, and love. I keep trying to

use the words that might appear on the page I am looking for.

I show my older son, Noah, how to make a compass.
I rub a needle against a magnet in one direction until it,
too, is a magnet. I slice a small piece of cork and balance
the needle on the cork in a glass of water. "Look," I say,
"the needle points north."

"Does it always point north?" he asks.

"I think so," I say.

"Even if it's broken? Even if the cork is very, very
old? Even if your eyes are closed? Even if the water is
too cold?"

Little pieces of cork stick to the side of the glass, like
children staring out a window.

"I don't know," I say.

"Also, Mama. You didn't have to use a cork. You
could've used a leaf. Or anything hollow. My teacher
already showed us."

I return to my childhood house. I am in New York
visiting my mother, so I take the Q. I get off on Avenue J
and walk behind a cloud of Yeshiva girls drifting and
thickening. Their long denim skirts make no sound.
Their chatter is as soft and crisp and serious as their
white button-down shirts. I walk behind them until I
forget they're there, and when I remember them again,
they're gone. The sky is higher than it was when I was a
child, and the streets are emptier. When I get to the
house, I imagine a miracle, but instead the house is just

a white house with dark red steps and a small front yard. No summer snow blanketing the trees. No crash of lightning. No hundred crows with small bits of black yarn in their beaks suddenly everywhere. It's just a house on a quiet street.

Go back home, says the house. *It's better for both of us.*

I don't come any closer. The next-door neighbor is watching me take photos. "I lived here thirty-five years ago," I yell from across the street. My voice is loud and hollow and dusty.

"Are you the doctor's daughter?"

"I am," I say.

"You wouldn't even recognize the inside," he says. "You wouldn't even recognize the inside," he says again. "Would you like some water?"

I would like some water. I would like a whole lake of water, and a boat, and wind going in the right direction. But instead I say no thank you. "That's very kind of you," I say.

I see the book of fairy tales my mother says never existed. It's just lying there in the front yard. The pages are weathered and thick as if the book had been thrown into a lake, rescued, and dried one thousand times. It wants so badly to burst out of its binding, it reminds me of myself, as a child, wanting to run away as much as I wanted to stay still enough to hold myself together. The crocodile on the cover reaches into the pocket of his brown corduroy vest and pulls out a piece of paper speckled with words. He crumples it into a ball. *Catch*, says the crocodile. And I catch. It is as light as I once imagined the moon. I will wait until I get home to uncrumple and smooth it out. I will read it aloud to my sons. Even if I don't understand a single word. Even if I imagined all of it.

HAPPILY

1

Ghost People

My son's teacher pulls me aside to tell me she's concerned about Noah and the Ghost People.

"Ghost People?"

"Yes," she says. She is cheerful, though I suspect the main ingredient of her cheer is dread. "Can you encourage Noah to stop bringing them to school?" She is whispering, and she is smiling. She is a close talker and occasionally calls me "girl," which embarrasses me.

"I don't know these Ghost People."

"You do."

"I don't think so."

"He makes them out of the wood chips he finds on the playground. They're distracting him. He isn't finishing his sentences."

"Okay," I say. "Ghost People."

She smiles wide. One of her front teeth looks more alive than it should be.

*

As a toddler, Noah always had a superhero in one hand and a superhero in the other.

Like the world was a tightrope and the men were his balance pole. Now he makes his own men. Out of pipe cleaners and twigs and paper and Q-tips and string and Band-Aids, but mostly wood chips. I eavesdrop. With Noah there, the Ghost People seem to speak a mix of cloud and wind. They are rowdy and kind. They comfort him. If Adam looked like anything in the beginning, I suspect it would be these wood chips, the color of dry earth. He, too, would be speaking in a language from a place that doesn't quite exist.

But also I know as Noah gets older the world will make it even more difficult for him to carry these People around.

"For god's sake," says my mother, "let him carry the freaking Ghost People around. Who is he hurting?"

"Maybe himself?" I say.

"Why himself?" she asks. "How himself?"

"They're distracting him," I explain.

"From what?"

"From his sentences."

"Who the hell cares?" says my mother.

＊

In Carlo Collodi's *Pinocchio,* the first thing Pinocchio does, once his mouth is carved, is laugh at Geppetto. And the first thing he does once his hands are finished is snatch Geppetto's yellow wig off his head. And the first thing he does once his feet are done is kick Geppetto in the nose, leaving him to feel "more wretched and miserable than he felt in all his life." If what he is making hurts him, why does Geppetto keep carving? Maybe it's because before he even began carving, he knew he would call his wooden son Pinocchio. Maybe because Geppetto understands that sometimes the things we create to protect us, to give us good fortune, need first to thin us into a vulnerability where the only thing that can save us are those things that almost erased us. Where the only thing that can bring us back to ourselves is what brought us to the edge of our being in the first place. Or maybe it's just that Geppetto is lonely.

"What did you do today at school?"

"Nothing," says Noah.

When I empty his lunch bag, I find three Ghost People inside.

In the world of fairy tales, Geppetto is the mother of all mothers. After jail, beatings, poverty, hunger, and crying, all brought on by his spoiled, lying wooden boy, he still—heartsick—looks for his boy everywhere. They finally unite in the belly of a shark. Pinocchio walks and walks toward a "glow" until he reaches Geppetto, lit by the flame of his last candlestick, sitting at a small dining table eating live minnows. He is now little and old and so white he "might have been made of snow or whipped cream." Promising to never leave him again, Pinocchio (only a meter tall) swims out of the shark's mouth, toward the moonlight and the starry sky, with Geppetto on his back. If an old man and a wooden boy ever shared a single birth, it would probably look something like this.

Eli doesn't make Ghost People, but his pockets are always filled with sticks and leaves. If I were to keep everything my boys have ever found and brought home, I could easily have enough for a whole tree. Maybe even a small forest. When the shooting happened at the Tree of Life Synagogue in Pittsburgh on October 27, 2018, all I could think about at first was the name of the synagogue. All I could think about was the Tree. I shut the news off fast.

"What happened to the Tree of Life?" asks Noah.

"Nothing," I say. "I think a branch fell."

I haven't yet read my boys *Pinocchio,* the story of a boy carved from a tree, and I don't tell them about the shooting at the Tree of Life, either. I get an email from our synagogue: "Join Us for Coffee and an Informal Discussion About How We Can Help Our Children Cope With Frightening Situations As Well As Anti-Semitism." I go to the meeting. At the meeting, one mother maps out the Active Shooter Plan she's drawn up with the help of her five- and eight-year-olds.

I say I've told my boys nothing. Some congregants say I'm keeping my sons in a "bubble." Another congregant, feeling protective of me, interrupts with the word *cocoon.* "Cocoon is more like it," she explains. What she means, I think, is that *bubble* implies a lack of air, whereas *cocoon* implies transformation.

"Her boys might not be ready," says another congregant.

Who is ready? I wonder. At forty-three, I'm not ready. Ready to know we can be burst into smithereens at any moment? Ready to be hated since forever?

An Israeli congregant explains he keeps nothing from his children. He uses the word *inoculation*. Like if you inject little pieces of horror into your children, they won't shatter when the horror comes.

I get his point. I shove a piece of cake into my mouth. I shove a piece of cake into my mouth because I can't shove the entire room into my mouth. Because I can't shove all the windows, and chairs, and all the parents, and all their fears, and all their children, too. I don't know how to save anybody.

When I pick Noah up from Sunday school, later that morning, an enormous paper *hamsa* dangles around his neck by a soft strand of red yarn. The *hamsa* is brightly colored and beautiful and heartbreaking. "It's for protection," says Noah. I watch the other Jewish children spill from the classroom wearing paper hands on their chests, too. "It's the paper hand of God," says Noah. He swings the yarn around so now the *hamsa* is against his back. He is so small, suddenly. He is wearing rain boots, but I don't remember it raining that day.

My child, I want to say at the meeting at the synagogue, *carries Ghost People around so we'll be fine.* I want to say, *I haven't even read my sons* Pinocchio *yet.* I want to say, *How many minutes of all our children's childhoods are left?* Instead, I say, "My children ask me if their Black father was ever a slave. They ask me if they will ever be turned into slaves. They ask me if I would ever be turned into a slave for being their mother. As Black Jewish boys, my children will never be in a bubble. But if there was a bubble big enough, I'd move there in a second." Everyone gets very quiet. "Tell me where the bubble is. Where's the bubble?"

*

In late sixteenth-century Prague, when waves of hatred rose against the Jews again, a story brewed about Rabbi Loew, who made a golem out of prayers and clay, a golem whose job it was to guard the Jews from harm. There are two versions of how the rabbi brought the golem to life. The first is that he inserted the *shem,* a parchment with God's name, into the golem's mouth; the second is that he inscribed the word *emet,* or "truth," on the golem's forehead. Unlike Pinocchio, the golem doesn't speak. Unlike Pinocchio, the golem doesn't lie. But he can hear and he can understand.

In a 1969 painting by the surrealist artist and writer Leonora Carrington entitled *The Bath of Rabbi Loew,* the rabbi is in his bathtub dreaming up the golem. The rabbi glows white, not unlike Geppetto in the belly of the shark. In the doorway, carrying a water jug, is most likely the golem in a nightgown. A figure wearing a hat shaped like a gigantic teardrop or a black lightbulb stands behind the rabbi. The figure is holding a towel.

Surrounding the bath are what look like the letters of an unknown alphabet or the footprints of Noah's Ghost People. It's hard to tell.

When the slander about the Jews using the blood of Christian babies in their rituals begins to quiet, Rabbi Loew decides the golem is no longer needed. In one story, the name of God is removed from the golem's mouth, and he dies. But in another stranger and more beautiful story, a little girl rubs the *aleph* off his forehead and turns *emet* into *met:* "truth" into "death." Because in Hebrew the only thing standing between truth and death is an *aleph*. In the *Sefer Yetzirah,* the oldest and most mysterious of all the cabalistic texts, the *aleph* is represented by silence, and its "value designation" is "mother." I wonder what would've happened had Geppetto given Pinocchio an *aleph*. A small one, carved onto the bridge of his nose. Because, ultimately, aren't silence and truth what Pinocchio is always missing?

Originally, *Pinocchio* was only fifteen chapters long. And in the last chapter, Pinocchio is hanged. Only at the behest of a pleading editor did Collodi save the boy. At the end of the expanded *Pinocchio,* the old wooden puppet sits on a chair with its arms dangling, its head bent, and the real boy Pinocchio barely regards it. He does not go to the puppet. Or fix its head. Or knock on its wood for good luck. He doesn't even have the kindness to speak to it. "How funny I was," he says, "when I was a puppet . . . and how happy I am now that I am a proper little boy."

Noah has begun making paper clothes for his Ghost People. It's winter, after all. I watch him cut out a tiny scarf and realize that I've never taught him to pray. I've taught him the prayers over the wine and the challah and the candles, but I've never taught him to pray. Or maybe praying isn't taught. Or this is praying. Or praying is keeping the Ghost People warm. The mouthless, earless Ghost People. "Faith" in Hebrew is *emunah*. It appears in the Bible as "to hold steady," but also as *eman,* which means "a nursing father."

"This one," says Noah, "has a fever."

I feel the Ghost Person's head.

"Is it a fever?" he asks.

"It is," I say.

He makes for it a paper bed. With a paper blanket. And a crumpled pillow, too. When there is a shooting, and then another shooting, and another, all the politicians' "thoughts and prayers" are with the families of the victims. "We don't want your thoughts and prayers," we say. We say this, of course, because it's the thoughts and prayers of men and women we suspect have (like Pinocchio) an *aleph* missing. We say this because after each shooting, it's already too late. The bubble has popped, and the Ghost People are already being buried.

*

My favorite drawing of Pinocchio appears in Edward Carey's *The Swallowed Man,* because in it Pinocchio's nose is a branch. The forking branch is the *aleph*. Right in the middle of his face, the branch is the silence and the mother. It is Pinocchio's roots. Carey's depiction of Pinocchio brings him closer to the golem than he's ever been. Also, the branch looks exactly like the branch I lied to my sons about. Like the branch that never fell from the Tree of Life. "What happened to the Tree of Life?" asks Noah. "I think a branch fell."

I look at my favorite of Noah's Ghost People and think about Rilke. "It remained silent," he wrote in his heart-stopping essay "On the Wax Dolls of Lotte Pritzel," "not because it felt superior, but silent because this was its established form of evasion and because it was made of useless and absolutely unresponsive material. It was silent, and the idea did not even occur to it that this silence must confer considerable importance on it in a world where destiny and indeed God himself have become famous mainly by not speaking to us."

I kiss the Ghost Person on the head. "What's your name?" I ask.

Silence.

"It's okay," I say. "I think I know."

More silence.

I don't know how to protect my sons. I wear their names around my neck on a thin gold chain. Sometimes I lie to them. Sometimes I say nothing. Sometimes I have to tell them that people do terrible things. Every day I send them out into the world, and they come home with rocks and twigs and wood chips and acorns and dead bugs in their pockets. It's been getting colder and colder here. If I could, would I have a golem sit in the corner of my kitchen, follow my boys to school, accompany us to synagogue, and stand at the door?

I look around my house. Maybe the golem is already here. "Hello, hello?"

More silence.

Maybe my house is the golem. And my neighbor's house, too. And the synagogue is the golem and the school is the golem. Maybe all the buildings in our town are the golem. Or maybe the town is the golem. Or the country, or maybe the whole earth is the golem. Here we are. Inside the golem. Knock, knock. Who's there? It's us. Us who? Knock, knock. Who's there? It's us. Us who? Knock, knock. Who's there. It's us. Us who?

2

The Nightmares of Horses

I wake up early so I can get to Yad Vashem, the Holocaust museum, by eight o'clock, when it opens. I am in Jerusalem with my family, and I have only one hour because we are scheduled to go to the Kotel, where it will be so crowded that I will never get close enough to slip my prayer into the wall's ancient cracks. It is Passover. Everyone is rushing the wall as if god were impatient, or actually there, and if there, then not there for long. Squeezed between too many bodies, I give up, walk back, and wait for my husband and my sons to emerge from the men's section with better luck.

A week later, when I get home, I will leave my prayer inside a Hebrew copy of Bruno Schulz's *The Street of Crocodiles,* also a holy ruin, a temple. Like most prayers, my prayer is for health. Eli tells me that since I didn't get my prayer to the wall, it will never come true, and so I imagine a long, imminent plague: pleurisy, and lice, and fevers and damp bedsheets, and thick rashes. But for now it is eight o'clock and I have only one hour. I leave my children with my husband because my children are too young to go to a Holocaust museum. We are all too young. We are all too old. When I get to Yad Vashem, I'm surprised I can just walk through the door without first swimming across a river of sour milk.

What I've come to the Holocaust museum to see are fairy tales. Specifically, the fairy tales that the Polish writer Bruno Schulz painted on the walls of a boy's nursery. The boy was the son of a Gestapo officer, Felix Landau, who offered Bruno Schulz protection in exchange for his art. I wonder what it smelled like in that bedroom as he painted. Onions? Blood? Newspaper? Fresh laundry? Shortly after the mural was completed, Karl Günther, also a Nazi, shot and killed Bruno Schulz while he was walking home with a loaf of bread. This was 1942 in Drohobycz, then part of Poland. The paintings are of Cinderella and Snow White, several shadowy figures including two dwarves, and a horse-drawn carriage. After the Holocaust, the figures receded like the dead and were painted over.

In 2001 they were discovered again by the documentary filmmaker Benjamin Geissler and his father while filming *Finding Pictures*. The discovery (in the apartment of a woman in thick glasses that seem to endlessly fog) begins as a hallelujah (as paint is carefully rubbed away to reveal faces) and ends in despair. As soon as the paintings are found, in a tiny pantry, behind onions and garlic and rose-colored paint, they are gone. Five fragments are removed by a crew from Yad Vashem, alleg-edly without permission. The question as to who owns Bruno Schulz—Israel or Poland—rises, as the dead might rise and wander wearily home, except there is no more home.

More of the mural remains in the apartment, accord-ing to Geissler, but now it seems no one can get to it. "The picture is destroyed," he says, "and nobody will know the whole picture." But for me this is the least sad part of the story. What picture is ever whole, what good plot ever tells all its secrets? Panning back, I imagine the whole scene to be swarming with fairy tales: the mostly blind Polish lady unknowingly living with dwarves and princesses behind her garlic, the Rumpelstiltskin deal Bruno Schulz struck with a Nazi (to spin straw into gold in order to stay alive), the monster Felix Landau dis-guised as a man, and the poverty and the shadows and the staircases and the cupboards and the misery.

When we say a story is *like* a fairy tale, what do we mean? Usually there is an evil stepmother, children on the verge of being eaten, spells, talking animals, forests, three wishes, three paths, three sons, magic eggs or beans or cakes. Usually there is hunger and a dead mother. Usually there is a witch. We turn to fairy tales not to escape but to go deeper into a terrain we've inherited, the vast and muddy terrain of the human psyche. Fairy tales, like glass coffins, like magic mirrors, give transpar-ency to the reflection of the human gaze. Fairy tales are homemade stories turned inside out. You can see the threads, the stitching line, the seams. Sometimes a needle is still attached to a loose thread, hanging.

My mother pricked me once on the pinkie with that needle. "It's so you never tell a lie," she said. "I hate liars."

"What about this story?" I asked. "About you pricking me with a needle on my pinkie so that I never lie? Isn't that a lie?"

"There is a big difference between deceit," she explained, "and using what is unreal to get to something even realer."

I stand very quietly beside the frescoes. It's just me and a security guard in the gallery. It is 8:05 a.m. I want to kneel, or whisper I love you, but a shyness comes over me. Bruno Schulz had painted his father's face into one of the dwarves', and the face of his beloved childhood maid into Snow White's, and his own face into the face of the carriage driver, hiding himself and his loved ones deep inside a fairy tale. I stare at the pieces of wall and imagine Bruno Schulz painting fairy tales to save his life, and I imagine Felix Landau (the father of a boy with fairy tales on his walls) shooting Jews in the head and the heart after having them dig their own graves.

I step back from the paintings. And then I take a few steps closer. I haven't yet written my prayer down. These pieces of winking, wailing, sighing wall are in themselves cracks, but even if there were a small hole in which to leave my unwritten prayer, I would never leave it here. I am confused. The paintings don't bring me any hope. They weren't meant to give me hope. They were meant to save Bruno Schulz's life. Like the poems Guantánamo Bay prisoners carved into Styrofoam cups using their fingernails and pebbles, these fairy tales survived by the skin of their teeth.

The longer I stand there, the more the security guard begins to resemble Bruno Schulz. Legs delicately crossed. A secret smile buried deep in his face. I wonder what he's thinking. *Who is he? Where does he come from?* I don't have much time. I need to get to the Kotel, the other wall. On my way out, the security guard high-fives me, and as our palms meet, the smallest puff of cinnamon dust is released into the air. By the time I leave, there is no telling Bruno Schulz apart from this man.

Jerusalem on April mornings is the color of bones under the thinnest veil of pink, leaving me with the sensation that I might be walking around inside a dried-out body. Or inside a book left open in the bright sun, for days, for weeks, words growing paler and paler.

The fight over Bruno Schulz's fairy tales suspends them in a Gehinnom, a spiritual purgatory. An afterlife filled with endless sky and no ground. As a kid, I grew up in two homes. One was my mother's. One was my father's. What I remember most clearly is the space between them. Like the father in Bruno Schulz's stories who "remained in permanent contact with the unseen world of mouseholes, dark corners, chimney vents, and dusty spaces under the floor," who put his ear to cracks

Bruno Schulz, *Carriage Driver* (Self-portrait), Drohobycz, 1941/42 Credit: Yad Vashem

and listened intently, I, too, believe the horse barely visible behind whitewash keeps more poetry than the horse on display. I recently read *The Little Prince* to my sons, and when I got to this line—"'What makes the desert beautiful,' said the little prince, 'is that somewhere it hides a well'"—I read it three times. Just in case it was a spell.

The first night I slept in my Blue House in Georgia, I had the worst nightmares of my life. And when I woke up, the only way I could describe the nightmares was that they were not human nightmares. I called my husband, who was not yet my husband. Barely divorced, he was living across town, suspended between the home he was leaving and the home we were about to begin. "Last night," I said, "I had the nightmares of horses."

"They were Civil War horses," he said, with the confidence of a man who was certain he shared my dreams.

"Civil War horses," I repeated. I put my mouth on the floorboards. "Can you hear me?" I whispered. "I don't think I belong here either."

I walked around my house all day unpacking slowly and thinking about what was buried beneath me. Sometimes I feel like the dead are the ones who move us around the world, like board game pieces.

"What does infillion look like?" asks Eli.

"Do you mean infinity?"

"Yes, that's what I said, infillion."

"I think it looks like all the things we cannot see."

In *Finding Pictures*, the Polish and Ukrainian experts who come to remove the paint from the walls to see what's underneath admit their inability to *see*. "I can't see anything," one says. "I forgot my glasses," says another. Anyone watching the documentary can see the clear outlines of Schulz's fairy-tale ghosts. But the experts cannot see. Not yet, anyway. One refers to a horse's head that is clearly a horse's head as an alleged horse's head.

I hear a lot of writers give this as advice: TELL THE TRUTH. And then almost everyone cheers. I don't cheer. I wonder, what truth? The truth of Schulz, or Landau, or his son? The truth of Yad Vashem, or the Polish government, or the cloudy-eyed woman who unknowingly lives with fairy tales behind her dry goods and her produce? The truth of my mother, or the experts, or the horse?

My stories begin with characters that are simple and archetypal, like the Stepchild or the Mother or the Father or the Husband or the Sister or the Sons. I found them all in fairy tales. But when I found them, they were cracked, and painted over a thousand times. I write words on small pieces of paper (sometimes prayers, sometimes jokes) and leave them in their cracks, their broken places. In return, they occasionally give me a story. I don't know whether I should admit this or not, but once I wiped away the paint on the Mother and saw my own mother's face peering back at me.

I have a recurring dream in which I find extra rooms in my house. One is filled with exotic animals, all sick, all waiting for me to nurse them back to health; one is overflowing with women in bikinis; one is bare but for a growing pile of dirty spoons in a corner; one has a perfectly made black bed, but when I sit on it, I fall. The bed scatters like static because the bed is not a bed but hundreds and hundreds of black ants in the shape of a bed. Even the bedsheets are ants, even the pillow. One room is long and narrow and lit by a row of open refrigerators filled with rotten food. A glass door opens into a garden filled with cobblestones and flowers and ponds crowded with old brown swans.

I don't want to be in any of those rooms. But they are cracks in my mind I slip through. One day, I imagine, I will have a dream in which I open a door to find the blind Polish woman standing there. Maybe in the dream her name will be Bruno Schulz or Sabrina Orah Mark. Maybe in the dream her eyes will uncloud and she will be able to see. Maybe I'll read her a fairy tale.

3

Rat-a-Tat-Tat

"I'm dying," says my grandmother.

"Dying where?" I ask. "I'm coming. Don't go anywhere before I get there."

"I have to go," says my grandmother.

On December 26, 2018, my grandmother, Gertrude Mark, died somewhere.

*

If this were a fairy tale, I'd go look for her.

My hair has been going slowly white since I turned eighteen. I color it brown, but a few months ago I decided to grow out one strand. Like snow. Like the cold, bright path I would take to look for my grandmother if this were a fairy tale. But it's not. This is America, and my grandmother is dead.

When my mother sees the strand, she begins to cry. "I hate it," she says. "I just hate it."

In Italo Calvino's retelling of the 1883 Italian fairy tale "The False Grandmother," "a mother had to sift flour, and told her little girl to go to her grandmother's to borrow the sifter." In other versions of "Little Red Riding Hood," the mother sends her daughter to Grandmother's with a loaf of hot bread and a bottle of milk. Or cake and a bottle of wine, because Grandmother is ill. Whatever the version, there are always woods between the mother and the grandmother, and the woods are thick with wolves. There is undergrowth, a rising moon, and the unsolvable riddle of choosing a path of pins over a path of needles. Like a house that gets smaller and smaller behind you, the mother vanishes from the tale once the story opens into the woods. And Little Red Riding Hood, like a streak of blood, is the trail that connects a gobbled-up grandmother to the barest trace of a mother.

I don't read "Little Red Riding Hood" as a cautionary tale of what can happen to a little girl who strays from the path. The path to Grandmother (like any good story) is by its nature a stray—it's rooted in strayness. And even Little Red Riding Hood, her name alone, is marked by a gerund: a verb disguised as a noun, a riding, a going away. I read the story instead as a tale about the wild space between grandmothers and mothers, and the child who grows there. In the Brothers Grimm version, "Little Red Cap opened her eyes wide and saw how the sunbeams were dancing this way and that through the trees and how there were beautiful flowers all about." The space between Mother and Grandmother is where the light comes in. It's where Red glows reddest.

In my grandmother's living room, my mother laughs at me for pretending to feed a baby doll my grandmother has just given me. I am five. It's my first memory of anger and shame.

"You ruin everything," I say to my mother.

In American author Kellie Wells's "The Girl, the Wolf, the Crone," a contemporary reimagining of "Little Red Riding Hood," the mother ("a soon-to-be-old woman"), who has a "loaf of bread always sitting in her hands," tells her daughter (Little Miss Red Cheeks) that she knows a "sickly wolf who would like nothing better than to receive stale bread from her." It's a genius twist. The mother tells her daughter to be careful because the woods are full of old women who miss the feel of bread in their hands. The girl is barely on her way when she sees "a crusty old woman with a face like a fallen cake" who is after the wolf and the bread and Red because Red's mother once "pinched the loaf" from her and "the embezzlement of fertility necessarily exacts a stiff tariff." The old woman (who speaks a mix of feral and ancient and, as it turns out, is the girl's grandmother) eats the wolf, who "unzips his coat and drags his body dutifully into her mouth." Then she waits for Red and her bread, and then dear Grandmother eats the girl and the loaf, too.

If menopause comes after menstruation, then what comes after menopause? In Wells's retelling, it is something wild and primordial and hairy and ravenous.

"A pagina," says my five-year-old son to my seven-year-old son, "is a cave covered in fur."

Good enough, I think.

When I was a child, a teacher told me that if you put a piece of challah bread under your pillow, go to sleep, and then wake up at midnight and look in the mirror, you will see yourself as a very, very old woman. And I did. And I saw my very old face, though I'm not sure whether I actually saw it or only remember seeing it. What I am certain of is that the very old face sees things. I wish to look out through that face, even if it isn't yet mine.

In fairy tales, you can open up a wolf and find an old woman. Or you can find an old woman deep in the woods in a hut that dances and twirls on chicken legs. Or sweeping with a broom made from the hair of the dead. Or living in a house made of bread with sugar windows and a roof made of cake. Or deep in the sea where no flowers grow, with her great, spongy breasts covered in fat water snakes. When you find an old woman in a fairy tale, often she is tucked deep inside the folds of an underworld where the psyche grows intuition like wild mushrooms.

For most of my life, my favorite activity was to talk to my grandmother. She and I would verbally line up every member of our family and go at them one by one. Subjecting each, without their knowledge, to deep analysis and Freudian cures. Looping and unlooping. Around and around we'd go. When my grandmother got to the heart of one of our relatives, she'd squint her left eye as though she were looking through a crack in the air. I wanted her soft wrinkles. I wanted her furrowed brow. When I was a child, I wanted to be old.

At the end of Angela Carter's story "In the Company of Wolves," the grandmother's old bones clatter under the bed like a haunted wedding bell. The girl lays the wolf's "fearful head in her lap," picks the lice from his fur, and imagines eating them "as he will bid her." It's a reception in a deathbed: half funeral, half wedding. It's a grave of love. "Since her fear did no good," wrote Carter, "she ceased to be afraid."

In my grandmother's final hour, her room was crowded with people, even though it was only my step-mother and my father who were actually there.

"She was moving people around," says my father. "Pushing some out of the way, and pulling some closer." My father is a doctor. "I could give you a medical explanation . . ." His voice trails off, taking science with it. In this moment, he is more a man with no mother than he is a doctor. And now that the world has run out of his mother, he wants to believe another more beautiful world has run in.

My father doesn't say, *Grandma died.* Instead he says, "Come home."

I feel dizzy and fortified and fragile all at once. It is as though I am giving birth in reverse. As though I now have a new, thick lining of Grandmother inside me, a hard soft thing. "Why is grief," wrote Gertrude Stein. "Grief is strange black. Sugar is melting. We will swim." Grief is the rat-a-tat-tat of a hungry wolf.

I dream I am flat on my back on an examining table. The doctor rubs a clear, cold jelly on my belly and glides a small rectangular box across me. *Look,* says the doctor. The waves of the sonogram echo as they hit a dense object, such as organ or bone. Such as my dead grandmother, who smiles in a small wooden boat. She is the size of an almond. Instead of a heartbeat, I hear a gentle splash. Her oars dip into my grief, which is now a lake inside me. The lake looks sweet and thick and dark. "This Water Water," says my grandmother, "has the strength of one thousand old Women Women." I look at the doctor, who is now Eli. He wants to know why I named him Eli. Around his neck is a bright pink stethoscope.

After the wolf in Paul Delarue's "The Story of the Grandmother" kills the grandmother, he puts her flesh in the pantry and a bottle of her blood on the shelf. "You're a slut," says a cat, "if you eat your grandmother." The cat never speaks again, and rather than reply, Little Red Riding Hood takes off her apron, bodice, dress, skirt, and stockings, throws them into the fire, and climbs into bed with the wolf. She outsmarts him by untying the woolen rope that the wolf tied to her leg and tying it to a plum tree. She outsmarts the wolf because she now has Grandmother inside her. But in Charles Perrault's "Little Red Riding Hood," the wolf not only devours Grandmother, he gobbles up Red, too. No huntsman ever shows up. Instead, a moral follows: *Be careful whom you listen to.* Tame wolves are the most dangerous of all.

At the funeral, the rabbi hands me a pamphlet: *How to Explain Death to Children.* He loved my grandmother, and he smells like old rain, and he is missing teeth. Every Friday night he called her before sundown to let her know the exact time to light the Shabbat candles. I look through the death pamphlet. Item number seven is this: "*Do not* give stories and fairy tales as an explanation for the mystery of death. Never cover up with a fiction or a confusing interpretation that you will someday repudiate. For example, to say that 'your mother has gone on a long journey' is to give the impression that she may someday return."

A week after my grandmother dies, we light Shabbat candles. Eli looks into the flame. "I see Grandma Gert in the brown part," he says.

"Unhealthy explanations," according to the pamphlet, "can create fear, doubt, and guilt, and encourage flights of fancy that are far more bizarre than reality."

"Grandma Gert is dead, isn't she?" says Noah. A week earlier he had given me clear instructions: "If she dies, never tell me."

"She is dead," I say. I am empty of poetry. *She's just dead,* I think. *I am the most boring mother on earth.* I scan my imagination, and the only thing I can find is the part where Noah never knows for certain whether my grandmother is dead or not. Like a white spot on his consciousness. And I begin to think about what might grow in this spot. A cold, empty, nameless thing. He should not have this spot. So I say it. "She is dead."

I comb many fairy tales for mourning rituals, but there are few. Death is often a spell to be broken, so to mourn as though death can't thin back into life isn't—in a fairy tale—realistic. Also, characters in fairy tales are never quite conscious. It's our consciousness that wakes them up, which is why the stories are so susceptible to retellings. Even in the Brothers Grimm's "Snow White," after the dead princess is unlaced and combed and washed with water and wine, the weeping dwarves cannot bear to "lower her into the dark ground." Instead they put her in a glass coffin, carry it up to the top of the mountain, and watch her body through the glass not decay. Snow White's glass coffin is the magic mirror her wicked stepmother has really been after: a magic coffin, a coffin of youth.

When the prince shows up, it's not Snow White he asks for but the coffin. "Let me have the coffin. I will give you whatever you want for it." The prince doesn't want Snow White or to solve the mystery of death. He wants the undying body.

My father covers all the mirrors with bedsheets to prepare to sit shiva. In the bathroom, I pull a small corner back, expecting to see my grandmother's reflection, but instead I just see my own.

After the funeral, we return to my grandmother's

house, where she lived for sixty-seven years. She is no-where to be found. It's barely been one day, and already the living room is windy and stale. "Where the hell did she go?" asks my brother.

For $6.99, a pattern for a three-headed Little Red Riding Hood Topsy-Turvy doll is available on Etsy. Flip Little Red Riding Hood over, and she becomes Grand-mother. Reverse Grandmother's bonnet, and now she's the wolf. I can't sew. Nor can I successfully follow a pat-tern without, well, straying. But as I imagine turning this doll upside down, then right side up, then inside out, I begin to realize that Little Red Riding Hood is a shared wolf song sung by a girl, an old lady, and a beast, about straying, and hunger, and dying.

At the funeral, the rabbi rips my father's shirt. It is a long tear down the left, over the heart. A frayed arrow pointing at my father's nipple because my father's mother is dead. I have never wanted to not die as much as I have since my sons were born. In the last photo-graph I have of my grandmother, she is sitting between my sons like twilight smiling in the middle of two dawns.

My sons don't ask me where my grandmother is now. Instead, I ask them.

"She's right there," says Eli. He points behind me at a bookcase where I keep all my old journals and the books my husband has published. I turn around.

"There?" I ask.

"Yes," he says, impatiently, "right there." He feels sorry for my inability to see, and then he puts his hand on my shoulder. "And also," he says, now soft with charity, "everywhere." I'm thinking maybe he should rewrite the death pamphlet. Number seven, close your eyes. Number eight, now open them. Number nine, now look inside.

4

The Bottom Line

"If we didn't have laws," I say to my sons, "we'd all be on the roof talking to the clouds." "But what if the lawmaker is bad? What if he hates us for no reason? What if he hates kids and brown people?"

I learned about the Nuremberg Race Laws as a kid in yeshiva, and I learned how those original laws to "protect German blood and German honor" bloomed and spread like a virus into more and more laws: Jews are prohibited from buying cake. Jews must surrender their fur, wool, typewriters, telephones, bicycles, cars, radios, dogs, cats, and birds. Jewish children are prohibited from going to school. And eventually, Jews cannot exist. I think I was nine. I had a dog. I would hide her, I decided. I'd break all the laws. I'd make sure my brothers always had cake. I'd exist.

My relationship to the word *law* has always been fraught. It's always reminded me of a yawn with jagged teeth. Or a large pink eraser that could rub me out.

"I don't like belonging to another person's dream,"

says Alice in *Through the Looking Glass*. The Red King, a chess piece on the checkerboard country, is asleep, and Alice has a "great mind to go and wake him and see what happens." When a country becomes the endless dream of a Red King, do we shake the king awake? Or is it best to let the Red King sleep, gently close the door, and tiptoe into the woods where things have no names, hold the trees, and pray we don't disappear? As Alice crosses squares that are brooks and streams marked by broken sentences and asterisks, the Red King never wakes.

Fairy tales are perched on a shaky turret of laws that seem to be both drafted and passed by whimsy and appetite. What keeps fairy tales from toppling over is that once the law is passed, the inhabitants of the tale stay under its spell until the spell can be broken. Until the dreamer wakes up. The citizens of fairy tales have lived under these laws long enough to know the tale they're in has stitched a *y* to the end of *fair*—it's a weirdly shaped wing that carries fairness away. The word *fairy*, from *fata*, is rooted in fate but lifted by magic. Here comes the wind.

In Giambattista Basile's seventeenth-century Italian fairy tale "The Flea," a king is bitten by a flea. When he picks the flea off, he is so moved by its beauty, he places it in a carafe and feeds it daily with his blood. The flea grows and grows. At the end of seven months, the flea is the size of a lamb. The king has the flea-lamb skinned and issues a decree: whoever is able to recognize the animal to which the hide belongs will be given the princess in marriage. People flock from all over. Is it a monster cat, a lynx, a crocodile? No, no, no. An ogre, "the most horrible thing in the world," soon enters. The ogre, because he's an ogre, guesses correctly, and since the king can't go back on his promise, he gives him his daughter, Porziella. This is the law of fairy tale. "Either you're a king," says the king, "or you're poplar bark." Porziella's face turns yellow. Her home will now be the ogre's home, decorated with the bones of men the ogre has eaten. "I can't go back on my promise," explains the king.

Fathers in fairy tales are not good fathers. In "The Juniper Tree" by the Brothers Grimm, they eat their own children without realizing they are eating their children and throw the bones under the table. "Wife," says one father, "this is the best stew I've ever tasted. . . . Give me some more." Only after the children return from the danger their fathers left them in do the fathers repent. Unlike the stepmothers, who pay with their lives, the fathers are usually forgiven. They are ineffective at best. Their hearts are clogged with forgetfulness. They are sleepwalkers. They wish to marry their daughters. Meek and docile, they obey the evil stepmother's wishes.

Porziella laments, "Oh, better if my mother had suffocated me, if my cradle had been my deathbed, my wet nurse's tit a bladder of poison, my swaddling nooses, and the little whistle tied round my neck a millstone, considering that this calamity was to befall me."

"Enough with your anger," her father replies. "Sugar is expensive . . . don't try to teach a father how to have daughters." If she doesn't shut her mouth, he threatens to "sow the earth with her teeth."

The fairy-tale father is myopic. He cannot see the larger picture his daughter is standing inside. He can only see the flea. Why is this? Why is the fairy-tale father a void? A hole an entire family might fall through? The hide of a forgotten law? Is it because the seed of the father, like a law, only grows once it leaves the father's body? If all the fairy-tale fathers were gathered in a moonlit field, it might look something like this: OOOOOOOOOOOOOOOOOOOOOOOOO.

Three years ago a doctor found a black spot inside my husband. We sent the report to my father, an internist, for a second look. The black spot was a law inside my husband's body I could not read, so I asked my father to read it. *What does it say?* I prayed the black spot had broken the law of what I feared. Maybe it was just a small black flower growing inside my husband.

"The bottom line . . . ," said my father. He always gives bottom lines. From my father, I have hundreds of bottom lines. I have collected them since I was a child. Each time he gives me the bottom line, I imagine the last three layers of ocean: the midnight zone, the abyss, and the trenches. Lack of light, continuous coldness, and few nutrients make it difficult, but not impossible, to live inside the bottom line, and yet the bottom line is a strange comfort. It's a place I can sleep when I'm drown-

ing. And some simple, beautiful organisms do occur
there, like snailfish and sea cucumbers. Bottom lines are
the cousins of laws, their long, cold bodies stretching
out like the only correct answer to a world we will never
fully understand.

Fairy tales are filled with bottom lines: the stepmother
is evil, the mother is dead, the lamb is a flea, the boy is a
bird, the Red King is sleeping, with a kiss the spell can be
broken, and whoever is able to [*fill in the blank*] can
marry the king's daughter. The fairy tale breathes in the
spaces above and around these bottom lines. The figures
in fairy tales live not because of the laws but despite
them, outside them.

What was inside my husband was not a black flower.
It was cancer. My father gave me the bottom line, and I
hung on to it like a woman dangling off a window ledge.
After the surgery, there were complications, and on
Rosh Hashanah my husband was back in the hospital.
The bottom line fell past its bottom. Noah stopped
sleeping. Eli grew quieter. My husband was hooked up
to a machine that slowly removed fluids from his body.
I don't remember the name of this machine, but I remember the sucking sounds and the green liquid like a
rising bog.

I remember the nurse's name was Alice, though I
know her name wasn't Alice. I wanted to marry Alice, or
for my husband to marry Alice, or for us both to disappear and for only Alice to remain. Alice, who could
take my husband's pain away. Alice, who opened the

heavy door of room 5777, which was also the same number as the new Jewish year, and let the light in. It was a year that began with diagnosis and ended in relief so big it felt like rapture.

The bottom line rippled and bubbled like a sinkhole and then, as if changing its mind, spat us out, and off we limped. The new law of my husband's body broke and set us free. It was like getting away with murder if murder was not dying.

My father flew from New York to Georgia to help us, as my husband recovered. "The bottom line," said my father as he walked into my house. . . . I threw my arms around him. The bottom line quaked. It sloshed around like stormwater in my throat: moonlit boo, nimble boom, omen bloom. "It's going to be okay," he said. Together we cooked a bone broth for my husband. All day it simmered and thickened. Occasionally my father stirred. The spoon he used was no spoon any fairy-tale father ever knew. It had a long blue handle. And when the broth was ready, it was from that same spoon my husband drank.

5

The Evil Stepmother

I am a mother, a stepmother, and a step-stepmother because I am my husband's third wife, and he has two
adult daughters from his first marriage and a daughter
from his second. And I am a mother-mother to our two
sons. "This isn't one of your fairy tales," my husband
once said to me during an argument. He didn't mean
Disney, he meant Grimm. He meant I was stowing myself in the body of a fairy-tale stepmother and setting
sail.

When all three of my husband's daughters are in our
house at once, I grow very small. The weight of those
girls who are not mine tilts the house and slides me
toward the door. The weight of my sons slides me back
in. Up and down goes this seesaw. My husband takes no
turns. He grows weightless and blurry.

On weekends, my seventeen-year-old stepdaughter
comes out of her bedroom in the early afternoon in a
thick white robe. She moves slowly, like a gathering
cloud. My sons worship her. She is soft and kind, and

they scramble all over her body like mice. "Play with us," they beg. She yawns. Shuffles into the bathroom. They wait by the door. Often she is in there for a long, long time. Her name is Eve, like the first woman on earth.

I love my stepdaughter, but I don't love being a stepmother. It's grim work. The stepmother swings like a lightbulb back and forth, causing the mother who is not there to glow. That is her job. If we stood side by side, Eve and I, and looked into the mirror, it wouldn't be our reflections staring back at us. It would be something wild and cruel. A discarded mother skin. A punishment for loving what doesn't belong to you.

When there is a stepmother in a fairy tale, it's because the mother is dead. She is ash buried under a tree, or she is looking down from heaven, or she is dead from childbirth. She is good and beautiful, but she should've known better than to have pricked her finger and let three drops of blood fall onto the snow, unleashing a metaphor for impurity. Because out of this metaphor grows a stepmother. A corpse flower in a field of daisies. A blooming shadow.

In the Grimms' "The Juniper Tree," the stepmother offers her stepson an apple, and when he bends down to take it from the apple chest, she slams the lid so hard, "the boy's head flew off." She cooks him up in a stew that needs no salt because Little Marlene, her biological daughter, seasons it with her weeping. The stepmother then serves the stew to her husband, who dreamily won-

ders where his son has gone as he eats him up. The father flickers on and off like an old bulb, while the
stepmother stands her ground in harsh light.

In Basile's "The Young Slave," the stepmother cuts
off her stepdaughter's hair, dresses her in rags, "blackens
her eyes," and makes her mouth "look as if she had
eaten raw pigeons." She tells her husband the child is
"only fit for the rope's end, and that one had to be forever beating her." And in the Grimms' "Snow White,"
the stepmother wants the huntsman to bring back Snow
White's lungs and liver so she can broil them in brine
and eat them.

It's easy to dismiss the stepmother as gruesome and
cruel. In fairy tales she always is. But I also read the stepmother's desire to tenderize, serve, and cook the child as
a way to replant the child into the body of the family. It's
a way for the stepmother to grow the child of another in
her own soil. It's about repossession and root. I get it. I
do. I mean, metaphorically.

I wear my sons' names around my neck on a thin
gold chain, but I don't wear my stepdaughter's. A friend
cheerily tells me to add Eve's name. "It would make her
so happy!"

My stomach turns. "I don't know if her name is for
me to wear." I am either a thief or I am cold-blooded.
"Her mother isn't dead," I say. "Her mother has a neck,"
I say.

"A monster," writes Colson Whitehead in "A Psychotronic Childhood," "is a person who has stopped pretending."

The stepmother is subterranean. In Robert Coover's novel *Stepmother,* she lives with her condemned daughter in Reaper's Woods with "witches, murderers, robbers, dwarves and giants, savage beasts, elfin angels, fortune-seeking boys and terrified girls, poor woodcutters, adventuresome tailors, lost minstrels, prophesying birds and bewitched frogs." She lives where things are both rooted and unstable, where "not even stones or sewing needles can be trusted to be what they seem to be," where bones sing and pots talk. She is a shapeshifter, too, both insider and outsider. "She has been wrongly blamed for evil done by natural mothers and weak or wicked widowers and is generally suspected of all crimes committed, even of crimes not committed but imagined."

My stepdaughter loves me, I think, but through a mother-ish fog. To stay comfortable she must dress for two weathers: a sundress (mother) and a woolen coat (stepmother). Our best conversations happen alone in the car. In a blur of transparency. With no windows open.

Should I even be writing any of this down? Am I committing a crime? I imagine my husband's daughters' mothers arriving in the middle of the night, throwing a sack over my head, and tossing me into the river. The earth's first mirror.

In the Grimms' first edition of "Snow White," there was no stepmother. She was added in 1819 so that any anger a child might have for her real mother could be sifted out and placed inside her. Like the lentils that Cinderella's stepmother commands her to separate from ash, the Brothers Grimm separated love from anger and good from evil. Originally it was the mother who was jealous of her beautiful daughter. Originally the fairy-tale mother in "Snow White" was two things at once. But now the real mother is dead and pure.

I love to clean. "She has," I overheard one of my husband's daughters whisper once, "a cleaning problem." Even as a child I loved to clean. At sleepaway camp, I would skip evening activities to be alone in the bunk and sweep. I like sorting. I like to disinfect and straighten. "When I am rich and famous," I say to my husband, "I will have my very own laundry room." I will have a special brush that will remove all the stains. I will line the walls with soaps from every land.

Alissa Nutting, a contemporary American author, brilliantly reimagines the Grimms' "The Juniper Tree" in "The Brother and the Bird." She describes a stepmother who "cleaned constantly, bleary-eyed in multiple hairnets, on her vigilant search for the impure." So often does she roll a vacuum that it begins to seem like a limb, and her hands—endlessly "beneath thick, yellow kitchen gloves"—have been forgotten. What the stepmother is trying to rub out is not the stepchild's impurity but her own un-motherness. The stepmother can scrub forever, but she can never get rid of what never grew inside her. And because the ashes of the first wife are buried under the juniper tree, she waters it with bleach.

I wish I were the only wife. My thirdness is a spot in the house I can never make disappear. When my son Noah was an infant, an old friend of my husband's stayed with us for a few days. She had known his first wife. "I remember," she said, "how beautiful she was when she was pregnant. Gliding through the house in a thin night-gown. It was practically see-through. She glowed." I felt sick. I held Noah tight as if the image of my husband's first child growing in the body of another woman might make us both disappear.

Mirror, mirror on the wall. Who is the motherest mother of them all?

I am also a stepdaughter. The first time I heard the word *whore,* I was ten. My mother's terrible friend leaned down, smelling like rotting chrysanthemums, her eyes flashing, and said, "You know she's a whore, don't you? You know she destroyed your family, don't you?" And yet, the night before my grandmother died, it was my stepmother who washed my grandmother's soft, dark, fleeing body. This is the opposite of a fairy tale.

The reason fairy tales last is that they allow us to gaze at ourselves through a glass that is at once transparent and reflective. They give us a double gaze to see ourselves from the inside out and the outside in, and they exaggerate our roles just enough to bring into focus the little pieces of monster that grow on our hearts.

The space between Snow White and her stepmother begins to narrow when she encounters the dwarves, who seem to suddenly spill from her like mothers, like children. A magical two-way birth. As the dwarves surround her, Snow White becomes both their unnatural child and their unnatural mother. This role prepares her for the glass coffin, an image born out of the stepmother's mirror. Now they are both encased in glass. And once inside what can so easily shatter, the stepmother and Snow White finally belong to each other.

When I was pregnant, I prayed for boys. I imagined my husband's daughters might forgive me if I had boys. If I had birds or mice or anything but daughters.

What falls on the stepmother's head at the end of "The Juniper Tree" is a millstone. A bird that once was the son—the same son the stepmother cooked and fed to his father—drops the millstone on her head and crushes her to death. What falls on the stepmother's head is the weight that comes with a child who reminds her she is never enough. What falls on her head is the reminder that she is a hollowed-out woman. A wind instrument that plays a faraway tune. I know this stepmother. I once came so close to her, I could smell the poison apple caught in the back of her throat. It smelled like jealousy and fear. Of never belonging. And ever so faintly, of love.

6

Sorry, Peter Pan, We're Over You

On the day before Halloween, my son's teacher tells me, with the seriousness of a funeral director, that Noah has decided he does not want to be Peter Pan after all this year. Noah stands close beside her, and he is dead serious, too, as if after she breaks the news, he will be the one to show me the pine box where Peter Pan now sleeps. The furrow in Noah's brow deepens, and I imagine planting in it ranunculus, heliotrope, chrysanthemum. Flowers we can pick to take with us when we pay our respects to the boy he has chosen not to be.

His teacher speaks in a hush. "He's decided instead . . ."

Shit, I think. Unlike Wendy Darling, who can sew shadows onto the foot of a boy who will never grow up, I can't sew. But weeks before, I had ordered the whole costume from Etsy: the green felt hat, the quiver and arrows, the tunic, the brown sash, the green tights. And now, at the last minute, a costume change.

"Instead . . ." she says.

Oh god, what? I think.

"Instead," she says, her voice growing dim, "he would like to be Martin Luther King, Jr."

I can't say no. I mean, I could say no, but then I would be the mother who told her son who wanted to be Martin Luther King, Jr., that he must be Peter Pan instead. What am I supposed to say? *You can't be Martin Luther King, Jr.—I already bought the green tights?* Or *I'd prefer you imagine yourself as a very, very old boy rather than as the most visible leader of the civil rights movement?* I was cornered.

It is already three o'clock. I need a black suit. I can draw the mustache on with eyeliner. I need black shoes. A white button-down shirt. I drop Noah home and run off to Target. I pass the girls' department, and a T-shirt flashes at me: THE FUTURE IS FEMALE. Sorry, Nibs, Tootles, Slightly, Curly, Twin One, and Twin Two. Sorry, John and Michael. Sorry, my sons: the future is female. Sorry, Peter Pan, we're over you.

I think a lot about boys. About raising mine to be sensitive, and effective, and tenderhearted, and lovely, and kind, and funny, and brave. I want them to be boys who keep their shadows on and who belong to a future. Boys who understand the difference between a thimble and a kiss. Worry picks at me like Hook's metal claw. I want their boyness to bloom. I want to keep them safe.

"Some idiot kid," says my mother, "probably told Noah he can't be Peter Pan because Noah is Black and Peter Pan is white."

"No, no," I say.

"Trust me," says my mother. "I know how this stupid world today works."

My mother is no Mrs. Darling. She is no Victorian. She knows children can be as innocent as they can be heartless. I sensed she didn't approve of the story from beginning to end. I wasn't sure if I approved, either. There is frankly something chilling about sending a child out into the world dressed like a great man in a stiff black suit who was shot in the neck at the age of thirty-nine.

On the other hand, it's Halloween, and this whole Southern town I live in is riddled with ghosts. So what's one more? Plus, it's no more chilling than sending your son out into the world dressed like a boy who at the end of the story can't even remember the fairy who drank the poison meant for him. Or like the boy who tries to stick his shadow back on with soap, then takes credit for successfully sewing his shadow to his foot, when everyone knows it was Wendy who did it with her housewife cleverness. God, I hate Halloween.

As I walk Noah to his classroom, the other mothers smile at him sweetly. Maybe a little too sweetly. My husband suggests he carry a Bible. We decide instead he carry a rolled-up piece of green construction paper that says on the outside "I Have a Dream . . ."

"I'll just be an owl," says Eli.

"Thank you," I say.

In J. M. Barrie's *Peter and Wendy,* the Lost Boys live

in a room at the bottom of hollowed-out trees, each tree custom-fit like a coffin. And at the center of the room is a Never Tree that tries "hard to grow . . . but every morning they sawed it off," like a boy who wishes to grow up but is stopped in midwish and turned back around. Neverland is as much a tomb for the unloved and forgotten as it is a map of a child's mind. It is a place ruled by a boy with a memory as thin as the skeleton leaves he wears.

Peter Pan forgets Wendy in midair, and he forgets Tinker Bell, and he forgets Hook. "Long ago," says Peter, "I thought, like you, my mother would always keep the window open for me, so I stayed away for moons and moons and moons, and then flew back; but the window was barred, for mother had forgotten all about me, and there was another boy sleeping in my bed." Like Mr. Darling, who locks himself in Nana's dog kennel as punishment for losing his children to Neverland, Peter Pan locks himself in childhood to punish himself for being forgotten by his mother. By never growing up, Peter Pan becomes the boy he is forever replaced by.

I look up Martin Luther King, Jr.'s, mother: Alberta Williams King. Six years after his assassination, she, too, was shot and killed while she played the morning service on the organ at the Ebenezer Baptist Church. Had I known this? Had I forgotten? Who forgets such a thing? Who forgets that Martin Luther King, Jr.'s, mother was shot and killed at her organ in a place called Ebenezer, which in Hebrew means "the helping stone"? She was shot while playing "The Lord's Prayer."

If all the Lost Boys live in Neverland, then maybe all the lost mothers should live in a place called "The Helping Stone." I look up Ebenezer Baptist Church's website. There is mention of Martin Luther King, Jr., but no mention of his mother. There is a job opening, and an order of worship. There is mention of the balconies and the stained glass and the organ, but not the mother who died playing it.

There is only one thing Peter Pan never forgets, and it's that he wants a mother.

J. M. Barrie, in his introduction to the play *Peter Pan,* wrote that he came up with Peter Pan by rubbing five brothers together, "as savages with sticks produce a flame." He wrote that he had no original manuscript of *Peter Pan,* nor even a recollection of writing the play. He describes himself as a shadow that follows his own body through a field at Pathhead Farm, digging up holes and unearthing islands he himself once buried. He scavenges, picking his own bones for its remains. Like the crocodile who follows Peter's ticking, Barrie follows a ticking, too. As if the splinters of boyhood left inside him might be the insides of an old clock he can hear in the distance. In only a few minutes he'll be exactly on time for the hours and hours that passed.

In Hans Christian Andersen's "The Wild Swans," eleven brothers are turned into wild swans by their stepmother. Their sister breaks the spell by gathering the stinging nettles that grow on the graves of the church-yard, and out of them she spins and weaves eleven coats with long sleeves. She throws the coats over the swans and turns them all back into boys. But she doesn't have time to finish the coat's last sleeve, and so the eleventh brother is left with a wing instead of an arm. Of all the fairy-tale boys, the eleventh brother is my favorite. I want him to let Peter Pan touch his feathers, while he quotes Carlo Levi in a strange and golden voice: "The future has an ancient heart." He might even say it twice more: "The future has an ancient heart. The future has an ancient heart." I want my sons to touch the boy's wing, too. To touch the part of the boy where the spell could not be broken. The place where he was marked by a Neverland.

I am making a list of costumes for my boys for next Halloween: Clock, Sleeve, Heart, Kiss, Hook, Spell, Wing, Shadow, Ship, Thimble, Organ, Stone, Stinging Nettle, Prayer, Island, Lost, and Found. They can each choose three: a first choice, a second for when they change their mind, and a third for what they'll never be.

Right before winter break, Noah comes home with a gift for the family from his teachers. It's a snow globe with his photo inside. Except in the photo he is not only Noah but Martin Luther King, Jr., too. His drawn-on mustache is a little smudged, and his eyes are shining, and the snow is falling. It's a very sweet gift, and he keeps it on his windowsill in his bedroom. Sometimes I imagine it growing wings and flying away. I crack the window open. But the globe stays still: the scene of my son dressed like a hero, surrounded by water and glitter, suspended in a Neverland.

7

Children with Mothers
Don't Eat Houses

Turns out, for three months, Eli had a small black pebble in his ear. Don't ask me why it never bothered him or why I never noticed. I am only his mother. When the very old doctor gently removed the pebble, Eli said, "Oh, there you are. I was looking for you all over."

About a week later I read about the Makapansgat pebble, a two-million-year-old reddish-brown pebble described as "water worn" with "staring eyes." In 1925 this pebble, a pebble with a face, was found by a schoolteacher in a cave in the Makapan Valley far from its natural source, suggesting that the pebble was carried a good distance, as one might carry a fairy tale, because in the pebble a human recognized something and so kept it and carried it.

In the Grimms' "Hansel and Gretel," it's not the breadcrumbs but the moonlit pebbles that point the children home. The breadcrumbs, eaten by birds, are the vanishing path that lead Hansel and Gretel to an edible house inhabited by a ravenous witch. At first, Hansel and

Gretel gently nibble at the house, like mice. Then Hansel tears off a big piece of cake-roof. Then Gretel knocks out an entire sugar windowpane. The children are insatiable because what they are really hungry for is a mother and their mother is gone. Children with mothers don't eat houses.

For my whole life, my mother has periodically stopped speaking to me. For months. For weeks. Sometimes only for days. The reasons are as old as the oldest fairy tale. As old as pebbles. I have betrayed her by disagreeing. I have spoken up for myself. She has slipped from the center of my attention. And now she has stopped speaking to me again. For days my chest feels like it's filling up with dry leaves. My head is bricks and glass. A shattering takes up residence in my body. I am middle-aged, and her silence still does this to me. I want sugar. I want to sleep.

In less than three paragraphs, the witch in "Hansel and Gretel" goes from mother to un-mother. First she feeds the children her house. Then she plans on eating them. She is as "old as the hills" because she is as old as all the un-motherish parts of all the mothers—since the beginning of time—added up. She is the stepmother's hatred of Hansel and Gretel grown older and more feral. A hobbling, hungry hatred. A blind hatred with a "keen sense of smell." What nourishes the witch are the children she despises.

"It's always good," says my mother, "to be a little bit hungry."

When I was twelve and my twin brothers were nine, we three lived by ourselves in our own apartment in New York City. We had a television on a cart we'd wheel around the living room waiting for *The Wonder Years* to come on so we could disappear into a family. And we had a frying pan. We had small hands that our grandfather would close around thick wads of cash. We had a father we saw on Thursdays and every other weekend. We had a mother in the penthouse, eight floors above us. We went to yeshiva. We studied Talmud. We stole school lunch.

My mother had bought an apartment in a building that would never be built. A home that went from endless scaffolding straight to bankruptcy. What was supposed to be a temporary arrangement, my brothers and I living alone, turned into years.

Now I live in Athens, Georgia, with the kudzu and the red clay and the lubbers in a house most likely built over the bones of Civil War horses. I have run away from everything that once was familiar. There are pebbles everywhere. Piles and piles of pebbles. Every day my sons come home with pebbles in their pockets, their lunchboxes, their socks. Like a thickening starburst, the pebbles make paths that stiffen in every direction. There are so many pebbles. They shine bright. The pebbles are rising. I miss my mother.

I mean to write about home, but I keep confusing it with hunger. I mean to write about hunger, but I keep confusing it with home.

Home in fairy tales is more like a parenthesis. A single curved bracket before a picture is hung.

If you stay home, there is no story. No pebbles, no witch, no oven, no water to cross, no apron pockets filled with jewels. Home in a fairy tale is like a cradle sawed down the middle, each half rocking gently on opposite ends of the woods. A cracked shell. The warm crook of two arms that will never know each other. What lies between is the hunger. What lies between is a child warmed by a small pile of brushwood that will soon go out.

One of Noah's favorite toys is a small brown bunny. His name is L.F. At first I think his name is *alef,* like the first letter of the Hebrew alphabet. But no, it's L.F.

"What does that stand for?" I ask.

"Lost and found," says Noah.

"Good name," I say.

Hansel and Gretel, left in the woods, believe their father is close by because they can hear the sound of an ax. But it's not their father's ax. It's the wind knocking a branch their father has fastened to a dead tree to trick them. To make them believe he is close when he's nowhere in sight. It's the sound of being abandoned. Even for a fairy tale, it's a blow.

The father's branch returns later as the little bone Hansel sticks through the barred door to trick the witch into believing he is not yet plump enough to eat. By showing him how a father can turn into the wind, Hansel's father teaches him how to be a bone instead of a boy. It's the lesson of a lifetime. It's what keeps him alive.

Over spring break, I send my sons to a camp for "creative rewilding." Their teachers live in a bus. Eli says his teacher's name is Jewel, but I find out later it's Joel. He has an arrow tattoo across the bridge of his nose, pointing east and west. If it rains, the children stand under a tarp because there's no actual facility other than the woods.

"What did you do today?" I ask.

"We learned how to walk through the woods like a deer."

I flash back to Yeshiva of Flatbush, 1983. I am eight years old. In a white button-down shirt and a long blue wool skirt, I am singing "We Are Leaving Mother Russia" at the top of my lungs. There are about a hundred of us singing into the brown air of the school auditorium: "We are leaving Mother Russia / We have waited far too long. / We are leaving Mother Russia, / When they come for us we'll be gone." The rest of the song is full of prison and the Russian sky, and dead boys, and passports, and freedom, and "another Hitler waiting in the wings." I rarely went outside.

"You have to be really quiet," says Eli. "A deer never ever steps on a branch." I did not know this. His face is painted with glittery blue ash. I can't tell if I've brought my boys as far away from my childhood as I possibly could have, or if I've somehow brought them closer. Closer than I could ever bring my own childhood to me. Which path of pebbles is this?

I grew up surrounded by rabbis. My sons are growing up surrounded by trees.

Sometimes I feel like I've made a terrible mistake.

"You need to get the hell out of Georgia," says my mother.

"And go where?" says my father.

"This is the most beautiful house I've ever lived in," says my husband.

"I wish we lived in Israel," says Noah.

"I'll teach you how to button your sweater," says Eli, "for when you're small again."

When the doctor removes the pebble from Eli's ear and hands it to me, I imagine pushing it into my own ear. As if it might whisper directions home.

It is a Jewish tradition to place not flowers but stones on the tops of graves. It is to keep the soul from getting lost. The Hebrew word for "pebble" is *tz'ror,* which also means "bond." Often, on Jewish tombstones, are these words: "May her soul be bound up in the bond of life: תהא נפשו/ה צרורה בצרור החיים"

Or as I like to read it: "May her soul be bound up in the pebble of life."

In Samuel Beckett's *Molloy,* Molloy (who is in his mother's room) cannot remember how he got there, cannot remember if his mother was dead when he arrived, or dead after, or even dead enough to bury. Molloy, who cannot remember his own name, has a thing for sucking stones and wants to establish the best way to distribute

the sixteen sucking stones he has to suck among his four
pockets so he sucks each stone equally. So no stone is
sucked less than another stone. "They were pebbles,"
says Molloy, "but I call them stones."

Are the stones the ancestors of Hansel's moonlit pebbles?

Molloy sucks the stone, then puts it back in his pocket,
but never the same pocket he retrieved it from. He desires
to circulate the stones with great fairness, as a father
might give bread out to his children. Did he forget to suck
one stone? Has he sucked one stone too many times?

But why stones? Stones are minerals pushed up from
the earth's core, as the earth's crust grows and erodes.
Stones are the earth's heart-of-the-matter. They come
from the center.

When Eli was an infant, I breastfed him endlessly,
while he rapidly lost weight. His latch was crooked, and
in my postpartum fog, I didn't realize he was burning
more calories sucking than he was getting from my milk.

"Maybe there's something wrong with your milk,"
said my mother. "Maybe it's making him sick."

Molloy sucks the stones so as to take every conceiv-
able path. But it's hopeless. "The solution," he says, "to
which I rallied in the end was to throw away all the
stones but one, which I kept now in one pocket, now in
another, and which of course I soon lost, or threw away,
or gave away, or swallowed." Right after this, Molloy
begins to see black specks in the distance: old women
and young ones, gathering wood, who come and stare.

One woman gives him something to eat. "I looked at her in silence until she went away." After Molloy gives up his stones, women like water-worn pebbles with staring eyes begin to appear. Women like too many paths that never lead to Mother. That always lead to Mother.

I am reminded of Lot's wife, who turns to stone—well, salt, a hard mineral—because as she fled Sodom, she looked back, perhaps for her daughters, perhaps to see her city one more time. She turned back and looked, like I look. She turned back to see what she will now forever look at without seeing. Lot's wife doesn't even have a name. And her punishment is horribly unfair. I wish Molloy could put his mouth around Lot's wife and loosen her out of her petrified state, out of her pebble-ness. I want to name Lot's wife L.F. A name that sounds like *alef* but stands for Lost and Found.

When the lactation consultant explained to me there was too much air between my breast and Eli's mouth, I pulled him closer.

When my mother's father died, my mother gave me his favorite sweater. It's the color of the woods in winter. The first time I wore it, I reached into the pocket and touched something hard. Three breadcrumbs. Maybe crumbs from the rye bread that he loved. I keep them in a small tin can on my bedside table. Eli's black pebble is in there, too. If they were children, I'd name them all. But they're not children. They're three breadcrumbs and a pebble. And they live where I live. They live with me at home.

8

I Am the Mother
of This Eggshell

When my mother's father was dying, he pointed into the gray hospital air and said, "Buildings."

"Drawn in light pencil," he said. "All around me."

"Are they yours?" I asked.

"Yes, they're mine."

Now he is dead, and his children are fighting over these buildings. I tell my mother I am writing about inheritance and fairy tales.

"Well," she says, "soon there will be no inheritance."

I imagine an eraser rubbing all the pencil drawings out at the exact moment my grandfather takes his last breath. An inheritance of rubber dust, as soft as the sawdust lining the twelve coffins in the Grimms' "The Twelve Brothers." That fairy tale begins with a king and a queen and their twelve sons. They are happy until a daughter is born with a gold star on her forehead. The king wants her to inherit the kingdom, and so he orders twelve coffins made. A coffin for each son, filled with wood shavings, and each fitted with a small pillow. He orders all his sons dead, but the queen orders them to flee into the woods.

What is inheritance? In fairy tales, it's where loneliness resides. It divides and isolates. It leaves the girl with the star on her forehead looking up at twelve empty shirts on a clothesline that once contained her brothers.

"These shirts are far too small for Father. Whose are they?"

The queen replies with a heavy heart: "They belong to your twelve brothers."

The girl heads straight to the forest and walks all day long until she finds the enchanted hut where her twelve brothers fled. They are happy until the girl picks twelve white flowers. What she imagines as a gift for her brothers makes the hut vanish and turns her brothers into ravens. She plucked from the earth what didn't belong to her. An old woman appears and tells her the only way to save her raven brothers is to not speak or smile for seven years, and so the girl finds a tall tree and "climbed to its top, where she sat and span, without speaking and without laughing." No one tells her to spin, and what she is spinning is left unwritten. Is she spinning a tale of forbidding silence? Is she a girl on the top of a tree spinning her new inheritance?

By the end of the month, my stepdaughter, Eve, will be living with us full-time. Eve's mother is moving, and Eve has graduated from high school with no clear next steps. She is lost, dreamy, and hopeful. Like the mother in "The Twelve Brothers," I raise flags to guide her. But unlike the fairy-tale mother's clear messages (a red flag for "flee," a white flag for "stay"), the messages on my flags are torn and blurry. There are days I raise none. There are days I raise too many flags while unfamiliar objects dot my house. I feel a quiet infestation, as my husband's second wife slowly empties her house into my house.

Soon my stepdaughter's pet tarantula will arrive. "Don't worry," says my husband. "It barely moves." Its name is Mavis.

Tarantulas have eight eyes, but they can barely see.

I am inheriting the kingdom, but I don't want the kingdom.

My husband once was someone else's husband. And before that, he was someone else's. When you take something that doesn't belong to you, with that comes an inheritance, too. The girl inherits seven years of silence and no laughter. I've inherited a girl, a tarantula, and little specks of meanness on my heart.

In fairy tales, when a stepmother cooks or banishes or beats the child, her rage is knotted into her fear of dividing the patrimony. My husband wears a small wooden juju, in the shape of a man, around his neck. When he lived in Senegal, a Ghanaian chief imbued it with spiritual protection and gave it to him. Breathing it in is like breathing in my husband, always as far away as he is close. He never takes his juju off. It smells like earth and starlight. In its torso is a dent that reminds me of the space between the branches that the girl with the star on her forehead climbs inside. A birth in reverse. My husband has a will, but I haven't seen it, and I don't think he's updated it since our sons were born. There is no money, only debt. But there is the small wooden man. I want not his daughters but our sons to inherit it one day. But which son? The juju is the color of lentils.

I look up fairy tales about spiders, as if I could use such a tale as a salve. A fairy-tale ointment I could rub on Eve's doorknob so when I turn it and see Mavis, I won't hate her. I find the Grimms' "The Spider and the Flea," about a spider who scalds herself while she and a flea brew beer in an eggshell. The spider screams, so the flea weeps, which makes the door creak, and a broom sweep, and ashes burn, and a tree shake, and a girl break her pitcher, and a stream grow bigger and bigger until it swallows up the spider and the flea and the door and the broom and the ashes and the tree and the girl, too.

I can't figure out if this is good news or bad news, and then I remember I am reading a fairy tale, not a will or lab results. What is a spider doing brewing beer in an eggshell? And whose eggshell is it? The flea's? The spider's? Mine?

"I am the mother of this house," I say to Eve. *I am the mother of this eggshell.*

Writing these pages about fairy tales and inheritance is like spinning a web. Sometimes spiders even eat their webs and use the digested silk to spin more. Maybe Mavis and I have something in common after all. But tarantulas don't spin webs. They are burrowers. Female tarantulas can live up to thirty years, which means it's possible Mavis will outlive me. When they molt, they can replace their organs, including their genitalia and their stomach lining. They can even regrow a lost leg. Mavis is the kingdom she inherits.

I am slowly beginning to like the idea of her. In preparation of Mavis's arrival, I watch a video of a tarantula molting. It sheds its exoskeleton like a ghost skin. Still itself, it crawls away from itself. The last time I watched a video in preparation for an arrival was a few weeks before Noah was born. It was a video on swaddling. On how to mimic the atmosphere of the womb for as long as possible.

Inheritance marks the place where one family member begins to fade out and another begins to fade in. I've inherited my father's legs and his hands and his sadness and his rolltop desk and his desire to fix everything. But the fade isn't smooth. It's a blizzard of static. A soft wrestle for existence. In this blizzard, the birthmark Noah and I share comes into focus. A dot above our lips, though mine is lighter. Like the ghost of my son's, or the half-realized dream of his more vivid one.

When Grandma Lila, my mother's mother, died, I inherited a ring that left around my finger a blackish-green band, like a thin swamp. The ring had been lost and then found. She died from Alzheimer's, and every night when I removed the ring and tried to rub the color off my finger, the smudge felt like her mind blurring.

I ask my father about a small mezuzah his mother,

Grandma Gert, wore around her neck, but he doesn't answer me. I don't ask again. I've inherited a terrible shyness of asking for what I want, but from whom I inherited this, I do not know.

Sometimes a check will arrive from my grandfather's estate, my mother's father. A visit from the dead. I cash it, filled with shame and gratitude. I sneak to the bank like a thief. Sometimes I don't even tell my husband.

About a month after Grandma Gert dies, a letter appears addressed to me in her blue cursive. I open it. It's a coupon for hearing aids. The font on the envelope is computer-generated, a cruel trick: BUY 2 GET 25% OFF. From my grandmother, I inherited the ability to listen endlessly. The coupon is cold and glossy. I rub it on my ears just in case it was my grandmother who sent it.

When he was alive, my grandfather received a monthly check for $1,229.54 from an Austrian bank. Holocaust reparations. Social security from a country that spat him out as a boy. That was his inheritance. I wonder how he felt cashing it. I kick myself for never asking, but he was a very quiet man, and I imagine he would've just shrugged. My great-aunt, his sister, receives a check, too. "It's like finding money on the ground," she says. *The ground,* I think. *Some ground.* The ground that once called us a plague of rats. Though we were more tarantula than rat. We shed our skin everywhere. A glowing inheritance for all of Eastern Europe to keep.

I ask Eve what she does with Mavis's exoskeletons. She tells me she throws them out because they are rough and hairy. *Like Esau,* I think, who sold his birthright to his brother for a bowl of lentils. I imagine sewing all of Mavis's exoskeletons together to make myself a gown. A stepmother gown. Something with a plunging neckline. A long, flowing, discarded kingdom I could wear while I wash my stepdaughter's dishes.

Or maybe I am the inheritance Eve doesn't want? My house is the hollow tree where she spins her story not in silence but in a language I cannot understand. In seven years, maybe the spell we are under will break. And I will go back to being the kind, beautiful mother with endless patience, and she will become the girl with a star on her forehead bright enough to guide her.

I live within walking distance of the Tree That Owns Itself. In 1890, twenty-five years after the Emancipation Proclamation, William Jackson left a deed that conveyed the oak tree entire possession of itself and all land within eight feet on all sides. The original oak fell on October 9, 1942, while trains overflowing with Jews were being sent to concentration camps all across Europe. A tree grown from one of the original oak's acorns stands there now. I imagine the girl with the star on her forehead and Mavis the tarantula and my stepdaughter and my sons and husband and all my dead grandparents eating lunch under the shade of this tree. A perfect kingdom. Where nothing, for a moment, is written out. Not even the silences. Not even the fear of being forgotten.

9

Rumple. Stilt. And Skin.

"I hope you're not afraid of mice," my friend Amy says. I am in her car. She clicks open the glove compartment, and a soft shock of fur and paper and string is gently exhaled. A mouse nest. "Hello there," says Amy. The nest is mouseless for now, but the mice will return to it when it gets cold. Eventually the mice will eat the guts of the car, a mechanic told her. But Amy won't disturb the nest. "It's their home," she says, shutting the glove compartment back up, not before petting the little nest that seems so alive, I swear it might be breathing.

For years I have kept a replica of René Magritte's sculpture *The Healer* over my writing desk. The bronze man has an open birdcage for a chest. A cane in one hand, and a suitcase in the other. Limp and flee, limp and flee, limp and flee. He is faceless, and his cloak is open. There's a hat on his nowhere head, and in place of his heart, there's a nook for doves to rest. Amy's car moves me the way *The Healer* moves me. Both tell a story of kindness and protection and ruin. Both will give up their guts to keep the vulnerable ones safe. Months later I am again in Amy's car. The nest has doubled in size. The car, for now, still runs perfectly.

Fairy tales are crowded with saviors: the prince on his horse, fairies, gnomes, godmothers, and witches. They appear out of nowhere. They are hidden, like the subterranean and the aristocratic, and then out of a clearing they arrive to save, or erase, or enchant the day. They are not angels or saints. And they are not without flaws. In German, Rumpelstiltskin (or *Rumpelstilzchen*) means "little rattle-ghost." And it is Rumpelstiltskin who can, unlike the miller's daughter, spin straw into gold. He saves her and even adds an escape clause to their contract because he is a compassionate gnome: if she guesses his name in three days, she can keep her child. He spins like the storyteller spins. And as he spins, I wonder whether the miller's daughter ever hears the *whir whir whir* in his empty chest. For his work, he wants what is missing. He wants something alive. No, the miller's daughter cannot hear the *whir*. She has cried herself soundly to sleep.

"I prefer a living creature," says Rumpelstiltskin, "to all the treasures in the world."

I wonder sometimes what the Healer would do if there were no doves. Would the Healer still exist if he were empty of the thing he was trying to save? Would he stand up and walk home? Would he disappear entirely? Would his ancient face slowly return?

In Italian, Rumpelstiltskin is called Tremotino, which

means "little earthquake." "All great storytellers," wrote Walter Benjamin, "have in common the freedom with which they move up and down the rungs of their experience as on a ladder. A ladder extending downward to the interior of the earth and disappearing into the clouds." Gnomes also come from the interior and can move through solid earth as easily as humans can move through air. When I write, I am rumple, and stilt, and skin. Everything is in disarray, and then if I'm lucky, there's an ascension, and then an undress.

Lately I have been hurting people I love with my writing. One friend (who is now no longer my friend), whose name I used in a story that was not about her, said to me, "I need to protect myself as a human being," as if the story I wrote had asked for a living part of her. I wasn't the healer's chest or the glove compartment as I had always hoped to be. I had always believed writing kept oblivion at bay, but suddenly I was accused of spinning it into a thicker existence. My fiction punctured my reality, and now I was the rattle-ghost that disrupted my friend's kingdom. "Tomorrow I brew, today I bake, / Soon the child is mine to take." Her name is not Rumpelstiltskin, though she did once teach me how to spin straw into gold. She once taught me how to write, and in return I hurt her. Her name means "enclosure." Like a nest or a cage.

"The storyteller," wrote Walter Benjamin, "is the man who could let the wick of his life be consumed completely by the gentle flame of his story."

Once many years ago, when I was writing only poems, an ex-boyfriend gave me a mannequin head for my birthday. It was rescued, he told me, from a children's clothing shop that had caught fire. The head was a boy's head. With singed hair and ash marks across its face. On the night he gave it to me, he told me he had fallen in love with someone else. I remember carrying the head home. I took the subway with it on my lap, too sad to realize what a sight we were. For about a year, I tried to keep the head in my apartment. It had already been through so much, and I couldn't bear the thought of throwing something away with eyes and a mouth. But it ate at me, this boy's head. It was hungry for something that hurt. It stared at me. I wrapped it in an old soft blanket, and moved it to the back of my closet. Finally I took it to the Salvation Army and left it there. "I'm sorry," I said. "I just can't."

How much of what I try to rescue is not actually the broken thing in my hands but the broken thing inside myself? The burned lonely boy, and the girl with no magic, and the doves and the mice. When I write, I spin a long, knotted rope. I toss the rope down. And it is me who is climbing up, and it is me who is climbing down.

A miller is also a moth with powdery wings. Moths cannot tell the difference between artificial light and moonlight. It's not the miller's daughter's fault she cannot spin. It's her father's fault. He trapped her "in order to appear as a person of some importance." And she's only a moth-girl with powdery wings. A nameless moth only two letters away from being a mother.

I have a dream in which Amy pulls the whole nest out of the glove compartment and tells me we should eat it. She holds it up as though it's a soft piece of cake.

"I'm sorry," I say. "I just can't. I have no more room."

"But it's your birthday," says Amy. "And you forgot to blow out all the candles and make a wish. And now nothing will come true."

My sons play this trick on their friends. It goes like this: "I one my mother." And then the friend goes, "I two my mother." And then back and forth: "I three my mother, I four my mother, I five my mother, I six my mother, I seven my mother, I eight my mother." And then my sons say, "Oh my god, you ate your mother!" And everybody laughs. Because the mother inside the body of her child cracks everybody up. A crack like a fault line that shakes the earth. And down, down, down goes the mother into the body of her son. Where finally she can rest. And feel safe. I'd be less afraid of dying if I knew I could one day be buried in the bodies of my sons. This sounds grim, but it's true.

Rumpelstiltskin dates from the sixteenth century and can be traced back to Johann Fischart's *Affentheurlich Naupengeheurliche Geschichtklitterung* (1577), which very roughly translates to "Glorious Storytelling." In it, Fischart describes a game called *Rumpele stilt oder der Poppart* (or "noise, limp, goblin"), which is like duck-

duck-goose except instead of a goose, there's a goblin, and instead of a duck, there's a man with a limp. The children take turns chasing after one another like goblins and scaring one another away with goblinish sounds. The objective of the game, as in so many games, is for the children to save themselves.

As a little girl in yeshiva, I remember singing about the Messiah. Hundreds of kids jumping and shouting. Our red cheeks glowed with a desire for a desire we were taught to desire: *"We want Moshiach now. We want Moshiach now. We want Moshiach now. We don't want to wait."* But I didn't want Moshiach now. Even at seven, I knew the only thing more traumatic than the Messiah never coming was the Messiah actually showing up. I had a hunch the coming of the Messiah would mean losing something. But I couldn't imagine what. Now I know that what I was afraid to lose was control of the spindle. I was terrified of being saved by a story that wrote me before I could even begin to write it.

There is a drawing of Rumpelstiltskin (by George Cruikshank) in which he looks like the twenty-seventh letter of the alphabet. A letter that should've come after *z,* but fell behind. When the miller's daughter tells Rumpelstiltskin she knows his name, he stomps his right leg so hard it goes into the earth. His lines are sharp like thunderbolts. He looks like a dying letter or an animal going extinct. The nameless queen and her nameless courtiers are standing around him laughing and laughing. Even the nameless baby appears to be laughing. Half buried, Rumpelstiltskin rips himself in two.

What becomes of Rumpelstiltskin? Kevin Brockmeier, a contemporary American author, describes, in his story "A Day in the Life of Half of Rumpelstiltskin," half of Rumpelstiltskin unspinning himself at the wheel:

> When the last of him whisks from the treadle and into the air, he is gold, through and through. He lies there perfect, glinting, and altogether gone. Half of Rumpelstiltskin is the whole of the picture and nowhere in it. He is beautiful, and remunerative, and he isn't even there to see it. Half of Rumpelstiltskin has spun himself empty. There is nothing of him left.

By saving the girl, Rumpelstiltskin falls apart. But what good is his magic if it goes unused? I sit in the passenger seat of Amy's car, knowing one day the car will stop running. And the mice will stop nibbling. And these words will fade like the marks on the burned boy's head. All of us are the whole of the picture, and all of us are nowhere in it. Our magic is also our undoing.

Rumpelhealskin, Rumpelprayskin, Rumpelpoemskin, Rumpelloveskin, Rumpelsaveskin. Rumpelsonskin, RumpelAmyskin, Rumpelstoryskin, Rumpeltruthskin, Rumpelpainskin. I used to think being a writer meant being a kind of guardian, a good guy. Maybe that was when I had enough of me to spare. Now I know better. It's about always being torn in half. It's about being dead and alive. An asylum and a danger. A rattle and a lullaby. Mother and un-mother. Saved and forgotten. A feral angel. A wing and a paw. Broken and sutured. I'm sorry. You're sorry. You hurt me. I fixed you. I lost you. You found me.

10

The Currency of Tears

One day in nursery school, when I was five I think, I cried. My teacher, in her floral apron with gigantic pockets, handed me a paper cup and told me to collect my tears, as they slid down my face, and drink them. "And when you drink your tears," she said, "think about your ancestors who were slaves in Egypt." It must've been close to Passover. She didn't intend to be cruel. Her face was covered with freckles the same rust color as the flowers on her apron. The other kids wanted to taste the tears, too. The teacher told me to pass the cup around. And I did. And from the little paper cup the children drank.

I wish I could remember what I was crying over.

In 2014 a story appeared about a Yemeni woman who cries stones. She produces as many as a hundred stones a day, and she cries most of the stones in the afternoon and evening. She is one of twenty children, and she does not cry stones while she is sleeping. None of her sisters or brothers cry stones. Her name is Sadia, which means "happy" in Arabic. The tears look like tiny pebbles, and they collect under her lower eyelids. It is not impossible that the girl's tears are the same pebbles Hansel and Gretel use to make a path home. Local doctors cannot offer a scientific explanation, but some villagers agree she is under a magic spell.

One year earlier, a fifteen-year-old girl from Bajel city, six months after her wedding, began to cry stones, too. In addition to the stones, "she experienced a swollen belly." And in 2016 in China, a farmer removed silvery white stones from his wife's eyes with a wire hook. The farmer and his wife believed the stones to be her tears, but doctors who couldn't explain the phenomenon called it a hoax.

I believe these women really were crying stones, but I also can understand their desire—the farmer's wife, the girl with twenty brothers and sisters, the child-mother-bride—to play a trick. How else do you call attention to your sadness? There are days I wish I could cry one whole boulder. A city of rubble. Glittering hail.

I don't cry as much as I used to. Maybe the headlines have broken the neuronal connection between my lacrimal glands and my limbic system. Like a petrified tree branch that stiffened and cracked. Or a blown fuse. I look at my phone and see this headline: COURT SAYS DETAINED MIGRANT CHILDREN MUST GET SOAP. Like water rising, my head fills up with it: COURT SAYS DETAINED MIGRANT CHILDREN MUST GET SOAP COURT SAYS DETAINED MIGRANT CHILDREN MUST GET SOAP COURT SAYS

DETAINED MIGRANT CHILDREN MUST GET SOAP COURT SAYS DETAINED MIGRANT CHILDREN MUST GET SOAP COURT SAYS DETAINED MIGRANT CHILDREN MUST GET SOAP . . . I can't cry. Instead, something hard and bitter has formed in my throat. I should stand outside a detention center and cough up something useful. No child would feel clean washed in some strange woman's tears.

In the mid-nineteenth century in the Bavarian region of Oberpfalz, Franz Xaver von Schönwerth visited servants, and laborers, and country folk so he could hear their fairy tales and write them down. "Nowhere in the whole of Germany," wrote Jacob Grimm, "has anyone collected more circumspectly, more completely, or leaving so few traces." Schönwerth published *From Oberpfalz—Customs and Legends* in three volumes, but the collection received little attention and faded into obscurity. In 2012, dusty, asleep, and half forgotten, these tales were unpacked from an archive in Regensburg, Germany, and translated by Erika Eichenseer. One of my favorites is "Pearl Tears," the one about Maria, the girl with a dead mother, a wicked stepmother and stepbrothers, visions of God, and an indifference to the stirrings of love. The stepmother has spent the father's fortune, and the family lives in miserable circumstances. One day Maria's stepmother and stepbrothers beat her so badly, she bleeds. "She retreated to the kitchen and leaning over a washbasin, she began weeping. Her blood trickled into the basin, and each teardrop that fell into the basin made a ringing sound. . . . She noticed something shiny in the basin and discovered some of the most beautiful pearls she had ever seen." Newly rich, the family can now return to festive times. Maria is so thrilled, she begins to laugh, and as she laughs, one rose after another drops from her mouth. Before long, though, the pearls are spent. So the stepmother and stepbrothers torture her again. And so she weeps more pearls. Eventually she runs away and lives out her days taking care of the poor and the sick.

Tears, like pearls, are currency. I ask Eve what she plans on doing (job? school?), and she bursts into tears and runs off to her room, where she stays for days and days and days. So I've stopped asking. "Let her be," says my husband. Snow White cries, and the huntsman lowers his knife. Cinderella plants a hazel sprig on her mother's grave and waters it with her tears. A beautiful tree grows, and in this tree lives a little white bird that grants her what she wishes. And the Little Mermaid would have cried, "only a mermaid hasn't any tears, and so she suffers all the more."

When I give the eulogy at my grandmother's funeral, halfway through, something happens. I don't cry. Instead, a sound like soot comes out, like a forest on fire. Burnt trees and smoke. Shriveled animals. I turn my head away and clear my parched throat twice.

My father and stepmother bring over an old cupboard filled with my grandmother's china and mount it on my dining room wall. It's brown with birds on it, and the teacups are blue. Sometimes I put my head inside the cupboard and breathe in because she hasn't even been dead for a year, and it still smells like her, and here I am. I look like a Louise Bourgeois house with everything showing but my head. A swaying *Femme Maison*.

"Mama," says Eli, "is just crying with her head in the cupboard because Grandma Gert is dead." But I'm not really crying. I just want to be alone with my grandmother. I feel around for my eyes. A little wet, but not wet enough. I wish my tears were feral tears. Like wolf tears with fur and teeth. Tears like a cold lake that has only ever reflected sky and trees. A lake so far away, it has never reflected a face. Not even once.

The fairy tale is a dead body that goes on living, which makes it impossible to cry over its grave. And if the fairy tale did have a grave, it wouldn't be a hole in the ground. It would probably be more like this cupboard I have my head inside.

Wild pearls, formed without human intervention, are rare. Hundreds of oysters and mussels must be opened and killed to find a single wild pearl. This is why the girl cries pearls and not pennies or diamonds. To cry a pearl means something living was cracked open and lost.

I wonder if, as with the Tin Man, all my tears have rusted my joints. I go to the doctor and tell her my bones hurt.

"Where?" she asks.

"My carriage," I answer, sort of pointing around my waist, but then down and then up. "Is that what you call this? A carriage?"

She is a very kind doctor, and the corners of her eyes turn downward like mine, like she knows the whole world is always on the verge of bursting into tears.

After blood work and X-rays, we conclude I am sad. "You're sad," she says.

"No," I say, "I'm a Jew. This is how we look. But also," I agree, "I guess I'm also sad."

She prescribes a small dose of Lexapro, which makes it even harder to cry. It is a round white pill, and from far away it could be mistaken for a pearl.

"Or maybe now that I'm fifty," I say to a friend of mine, "I've run out of crying."

She says, "You're not fifty. You're nowhere near fifty."

But I am near fifty. Nearer than I've ever been.

I wonder if tears have ghosts. I recently read somewhere that trees cry. If we can count on anything remembering everything, isn't it the earth? A tear is a hurricane. It's all the water on its way back home.

When my sons cry, I hold them and say, *Don't cry, don't cry, don't cry, don't cry,* when really I should say, *Cry, cry, cry,* or I should just hold them and say nothing. I save all their teeth, but I don't save their tears.

When I was a kid, I remember asking my father why newscasters didn't cry while they reported hurricanes, and wars, and fires, and dead children, and starvation, and injustice, and murder, and rape. And even now I am still always half expecting reporters to burst, and the screen to fill up with salt water and waves. Driftwood and fish bones. Crying as old as the oceans. Once a newscaster did cry while breaking the news on "tender age shelters," where babies would be held after being taken from their parents under 2018 immigration laws. "Put up a graphic of this?" she asked. But there was no graphic. They couldn't cut away. The only graphic available was the newscaster crying.

The preferred weight measurement used for pearls is the *momme,* a traditional Japanese unit equaling 3.75 grams. The preferred weight measurement used for loose tears is the "mother" or the "mama." I made that up, of course. My sons cry every day. Some of those tears are mine, and some of my tears are theirs, and some are my mother's, and some of my mother's tears are her mother's tears, and her mother before her, and her mother before her.

Crying in fairy tales is like one gigantic tear, hardened into a swing for all human sadness to rise and fall. Back and forth. Back and forth. A glistening swing pulled back by all the mothers who let go, and send their children into the air. A whooshing sob made out of the place where abandonment and liberation overlap, and punctuated by a mother fading backward into the distance.

For two hundred euros, you can order a Tear Collection Kit from Maurice Mikkers, an artist and medical laboratory analyst based in the Netherlands, and have your tears imaged into a work of art. The project is called Imaginarium of Tears, and the tears collected under a microscope look like ancient moons covered in starfish and grass. They look like the letters of a future alphabet. They look like thumbprints and battlefields and secret planets. I wish I could send in the first tears my sons shed. And the last tears my grandmother shed. Because I want to keep everything. I want to hold everything in. And then I want to let it all go.

11

A Bluebeard of Wives

"Sabrina," says my husband's first wife, "is married to my husband." I hear this through the Grapevine, a multibranched root system resembling the hearts of my husbands' two ex-wives planted in the same plot of deep, fertile soil. Vines like earthy veins, growing tough and twisty. A friend brings me cuttings. I hold them to my ear and listen.

I tell my husband I am writing about Bluebeard.

"Oh fuck," he says.

I look in the mirror. I have become uglier and stronger. I look out the window. A white shed glows in my yard. I live in what Angela Carter calls "the unguessable country of marriage."

"Bluebeard" first appeared in the seventeenth-century *Tales of Mother Goose* by Charles Perrault. A man with a blue beard, several missing wives whom he had killed himself, and extraordinary wealth gives his newest wife all the keys to all the doors of his very fine house. "Open anything you want. Go anywhere you wish," except, he says, for the "little room."

I ask my husband to clean out the garage, but instead, while I am gone for the summer with our sons, he builds in our backyard—dead center—a white shed. As the walls go up, his second wife drops Eve off to live with us, possibly forever. She also drops off many boxes. Contents unknown. The garage is half-empty now. The shed is half-full.

I call my mother. "Now there's a shed in my yard," I say.

"Of course there's a shed," says my mother. "Better check it for wives."

There are doors no third wife should ever open.

My husband, possibly the gentlest man on earth, came to me in a coat of old vows. I married him knowing he arrived with ex-wives. Maybe I married him a little bit *because* the vows had somehow deepened the lines on his face. Like handwriting I wanted to read but never could. I married him knowing, but I didn't know the wives would keep growing in a locked room in my heart. Sometimes they move around, angrily. Sadly. Wives, like peeling wallpaper. Curling wives. Wives like skin. Wives who tell their daughters things that their daughters, my husband's daughters, don't tell me. That silence breathes inside me.

"What did she say?" I am always asking.

"What did who say?" my husband answers.

"Perhaps," wrote Angela Carter, "in the beginning,

there was a curious room, a room like this one, crammed with wonders; and now the room and all it contains are forbidden you, although it was made just for you, had been prepared for you since time began, and you will spend all your life trying to remember it."

I am not an incredibly jealous person, but it hurts to think of my husband saying, "I do. I do. I do."

Once a month, for over a year, I am told that my husband's first wife is moving to our town any day now, but she never does. It's like when my sons put silver spoons under their pillows hoping it would snow in Georgia. Neither the snow nor the wife ever comes. Except for once. But it wasn't snow, it was hail.

"That's a terrible comparison," says my mother. "Wives? Snow? Who is putting what under whose pillow? Who wants the wives to come? You?"

Marriage is hard. There are days when all the dead wives are me. The wife who is never sad. Dead. Hanging on a hook. The wife with a good-paying job. Dead. The wife with a clean garage and a window that looks out her kitchen. Dead. The dancing wife. Dead. The famous wife. The wife with straight teeth. The wife who throws sparkling dinner parties filled with brilliant poets. Dead, dead, dead.

What do you call more than one wife? A bluebeard of wives?

For a marriage to survive, pieces of the tale need to be left out. I prick a pinhole through the story so I don't go blind staring directly at the sun. The deleted text message. The old regret. The surrender. My husband and I have been married for ten years. Longer than he'd been married to the other two wives, but not collectively. I don't want my sons anywhere near the wives. As if they'd fall in, and I wouldn't be there to jump in and save them. "'Sinkhole' and 'quagmire' are not flattering ways of speaking about other women," wrote Margaret Atwood in "Bluebeard's Egg," "but this was at the back of Sally's mind."

Few fairy tales have as rich an afterlife as "Bluebeard." Sometimes it's a bloody key, sometimes a withering flower, or an egg, or a rotten apple, or a heart-shaped mark on the forehead that is proof of the wife's disobedience. Sometimes it's the mother with her "black skirts tucked up around her waist" who saves the last wife from decapitation. "A crazy, magnificent horsewoman in widow's weeds." Sometimes it's a dragoon and a musketeer. Sometimes it's the wife who saves herself.

Like marriage, the cultural resilience of "Bluebeard" is mystifying. And like a fairy tale, marriage belongs to a never-ending circulation of happily-ever-afters in the shape of a cliff. I rummage through a big box of gowns and beards. Someone has worn these before. Now my husband wears the beard. Now I wear the gown. I do. He does. We wear it like skin.

In Angela Carter's "The Bloody Chamber," the matrimonial bed of the marquis and his nameless wife is surrounded by so many mirrors that when the marquis undresses his new bride, she sees dozens of husbands undressing dozens of wives. And when the marquis tells her to prepare for her death, "twelve young women combed out twelve listless sheaves of brown hair in the mirrors." On the edge of sex and death, the wife multiplies. She becomes the army of wives coming up over the hill. Are they coming to save her or to join her? It's hard to know.

I shouldn't be writing any of this down. It is not a good idea. These pages are the bloody key. It's my act of disobedience.

In the 1812 "Bluebeard," published in *Grimms' Fairy Tales,* Wilhelm Grimm (in the annotations) made a handwritten comment that Bluebeard believed the blood of his wives could cure his beard of its blue. This is why the wives' blood is collected in basins. He bathes in it. His dead wives are his medicine. An imaginary disease needs an unimaginable cure. "Magic," wrote the folklore scholar Maria Tatar, "happens on the threshold of the forbidden."

I look through old photographs of my husband. In one, he is with his second wife and their newborn daughter, Eve, who is asleep on a pillow. The pillowcase is gray and white, and I recognize it as the same soft, worn pillowcase I now sleep on. Have slept on for years. My head fills up with hot static. A biting shame. I pull the pillowcase off and put it with the rags. I should give it to my stepdaughter, but I don't, and I don't know why I don't. I just don't.

I am married to a man I love very much who had

many lives before the life I now share with him. Sometimes I look around for myself in those lives. Under the bed. Behind a tree. One day I might just jump out, whispering *boo*.

Or maybe the wives should put me in a barrel stuck full of nails and roll me downhill into the river.

The first time I met my husband's father was at his funeral. The casket was open. To this day, my husband's father is the only dead person I have ever laid eyes on. Our son Noah would have his eyes, his mouth, but I didn't know this yet. After my husband gave the eulogy, but before he could return to the nave, my husband's first wife flew toward him like a soft white bat. A blur in the air that had been locked in a chamber for years. She collapsed into his arms. Shaking and sobbing and coming into focus, as if she were returning to life. I sat in the pew like a dumb little girl. They shared grief, and they shared daughters. And at the time they broke each other's hearts, I was still nothing but a child.

If Bluebeard's wives were killed for having laid their eyes on all the dead wives who came before them, then why did the first wife die? What could she have seen?

At the funeral, I say hello to the first wife. She just stands there. Doesn't say hello back. Just looks at me. I don't know what to do so I hug her. And there we are. In each other's arms. Swaying in a church. She is old enough to be my mother.

This is how you make a chain of paper wives: Cut a piece of paper lengthwise. Fold it into quarters, accordion-style. Draw half a wife on the top layer. Cut the wife out and unfold. Voilà. A chain of paper wives holding hands.

I'm the wife all the way at the end of the paper chain. I look to the left down the long hallway. I see the little room. The little room where writing is safe. Here is the combination: key, flower, egg, apple, heart. I open the door. I go in. Look at this place. It smells like being alive. If I could do it all over again, I'd marry my husband in this little room. I'd give birth to my sons in this room. I'd die in this room. I would. I will. I do.

12

I Am the Tooth Fairy

"I know you're the tooth fairy." Noah looks me dead in the eye. We are out to dinner. A large television hangs from the wall. Without blinking, he looks back up at the screen. A small, dry wing falls from my back and lands on the floor like a candy wrapper. The thing about not existing is that sometimes it's a lot like being a mother.

"Sorry, Mama," says Eli. He pats my hand and takes a bite of broccoli.

I think about all the elaborate notes in pink cursive, the one hundred shiny pennies in a cloth pouch, the blue stuffed cat, the five-dollar bill, the Superman, the glitter trails, the wooden hearts, the breath I held, the way I ever so gently lifted the pillow, the sparkle-stamped envelope with the tooth fairy's address: *12345 Tooth Fairy Lane, Moutharctica, Earth*. I kept myself secret. I tiptoed. I used my imagination, and now I've been caught.

Noah looks at me again with a mix of sadness and pity and suspicion. I turn around to see what he's watching. It's a cartoon about a sea sponge who lives with his meowing pet snail.

A little light goes out inside me. But I can't locate exactly what it ever lit up.

After Tinker Bell drinks the poison Hook left for Peter Pan, and her wings can barely carry her, and her light starts fading, and after she lets Peter Pan's tears run over her finger, she realizes "she can get well again if children believed in fairies." "Clap your hands; don't let Tink die," says Peter Pan. Many children clapped, some didn't, "a few little beasts hissed." Tink, of course, is saved. She flashes "more merry and impudent than ever." It doesn't even occur to her to thank the children who believed. Tink, whose name sounds like a penny tossed into a glass. Tink, whose name sounds like a wish that won't come true.

Often as a mother, I am in a cold sweat juggling whimsy and delight. "Magic anyone? Endless fun? Astounding joy?"

"No," say my sons, "we're good."

And they are. It's me who isn't good. It's me who wants it. And I don't even want it.

What I want is my sons' illegible, lyrical teeth. I want to turn them into an alphabet just for us. Letters with crowns and necks and roots. Milk letters. Deciduous letters. In this language, I would draw a map that clearly marks where my sons' wonder is buried so they always know where to go on their coldest days.

Clap your hands; don't let Mother die. My sons clap their hands, and I brighten.

I've never seen a fairy. I've never looked up and seen a faint green glow. The closest I've ever come was once as a child—in a dream—I ran after myself, and when I caught up to me and turned around, I wasn't there.

We take shelter in children to escape oblivion. We ask the child to drag around the unwieldy weight of magic. To clap wildly. To believe in what we believe in no longer. We ask the child to keep the awe we forgot how to hold. The fairy isn't the fairy. It's the child who is the fairy. It's the child who is enchanted, a metaphor. My sons keep bursting out of their skin. They smell like poppies, warm earth, milk. And then one day, out of nowhere, they won't anymore. They are losing their baby teeth at what seems an alarming rate. Adult teeth bloom in their mouths. Their limbs grow longer and longer like shadows.

For whom is a child's childhood? I think it's for all of us. But it's not for when we are children. Our childhoods are for later.

Some believe fairies are the discarded gods of the oldest faiths. Like shed skins of light. They continue to exist because they believe, like a child, that they exist.

The fairy isn't the fairy. The mother is the fairy. The fairy flits back and forth, uncatchable. Who is she? The fairy is the space between knowing and not knowing. It's the realization as it dawns. It's what glows between a mother and her child. It's Puck sweeping the dust with a broom behind the door. The fairy is the dust. The fairy is the door.

In 1691 Robert Kirk, a minister in the Church of Scotland, wrote a treatise claiming fairies were as real as you or me. It wasn't published, though, until 1851, when *The Secret Commonwealth* was printed in a limited edition of a hundred copies. We each, he wrote, have a fairy counterpart, a co-walker, an echo. He described fairies as "somewhat of the nature of a condensed cloud and best seen in twilight." Their bodies are spongeous and thin. "They are sometimes heard to bake bread." "They speak but little and that by way of whistling—clear, not rough." "They hang between the nature of God, and the nature of man." Their body is "as a sigh is."

They do not curse, but among their common faults are "Envy, Spite, Hypocrisy, lying, and dissimulatione." They are prone to sadness because of their pendulous state. They can cure a sick cow. They steal milk, and when they are very angry, they spoil it.

On May 14, 1692, Reverend Kirk took a walk in his nightgown on the fairy hill beside the manse. Later that evening, on the same hill, his body was found dead. The body that was buried, according to locals, was a changeling. The fairies had kidnapped the minister in his nightgown, replaced him with a dead fairy, and held the reverend captive in Fairyland.

The punishment, it seems, for believing too much in fairies is to be snatched away by them for eternity.

Three days after I give birth to Noah, I am nursing

him in a soft beige rocking chair when a goat walks in. "Hello," I say. The goat, being a goat, says nothing. Most likely, I am hallucinating from no sleep. Most likely, a little piece of this world has torn, and through the rip, a goat has walked in. The goat lays his soft head on Noah's head, like a kiss. The room fills up with wild-flowers and then empties of wildflowers, and then the goat is gone. Who am I to say there is no thin veil be-tween this world and Fairyland? I know this now, but I didn't know it then: I am the tooth fairy.

This is how you can tell if your baby has been re-placed by a changeling: Boil water in an eggshell. If your baby is a changeling, it will laugh and reveal it's as old as the forest. In all its years, it will say when it suddenly begins to speak, it has never seen anyone boil water in an eggshell. If you wish to keep the fairies away, put the Bible, a piece of bread, or iron in your child's bed. And if you wish to see a fairy, take the rope that once bound a corpse to a bier and tie it around your waist. Bend over and look between your legs. A procession of fairies will appear. If the wind changes directions while you do this, it is possible you will drop down dead.

There are two kinds of fairies. There are the "troop-ing" fairies, who live together on a hill. And then there are the ones who attach themselves to individuals, like a haunt. If I were a fairy, I'm certain I'd be the second kind, but to tell you the truth, I'd make a terrible fairy. A terrible mother fairy who writes about fairies, and by doing so angers them all.

We are at the pediatric dentist because Eli has flown off his scooter and landed on his face. The dentist, who looks more like a very old child dressed up as a dentist than an actual dentist, puts Eli in a chair and raises it with a crank to the ceiling. She climbs up a ladder, and examines him in the air.

"You okay?" I call out from down here. From all the way down here.

She tells me his two front teeth will have to be pulled. "Bad news," she says, smiling. She lowers Eli and climbs back down. She hands me a brochure on sedation options. She is wearing tiny pink sneakers.

I imagine a back room filled with sparkling white teeth. Nightly she grinds them. And stirs the powder into her warm milk. Unlike the rest of us, she will live forever.

"Can we err on the side of nature?" I ask.

"I don't recommend that," says the dentist who clearly was once a fairy.

She shows me two fake front baby teeth attached to a wire. After she pulls Eli's teeth, she can "cement the device into his mouth," she says. "I made one for my daughter," she says, her red cheeks glowing.

The dentist's office is decorated like an amusement park: vending machines filled with toys, televisions frantic with cartoons, posters of wide-eyed animals in pants. The instruments on the dentist's tray—forceps, mouth mirror, periodontal probe—shine as the only reminder of where we are. There is even a giant stuffed panda. All you need to do is leave your name and number on a small piece of paper for the chance to win. I am so distraught, I almost enter. Would she deliver the panda herself? Would she knock on our door with the prize and then devour us?

"Let's get out of here," I say to Eli.

"Let's run, Mama," says Eli.

And we run. We run home, where it's safe. Eli's baby teeth stay in for another year. And when they fall out naturally, I add them to the rest. Between Noah and Eli, I have twelve. Twelve teeth. Sometimes I just hold them. Noah's in one hand. Eli's in the other. Proof of their babyhood. Proof of the mouths they left behind. Those baby mouths that spoke words thickly accented by the land they came from. Maybe it's those teeth that are the fairies. The ones the children, in order to grow, must cast off. The teeth that made little holes in the air with new breath.

13

The Silence of Witches

I have a dream my mother is standing at my front door crying. Her hair is wet and tangled in seashells. She's read a story I've written. "How could you," she says. "Your own mother." She opens her coat, and out march my husband, his daughters, my brothers, my sons, my father. I try to run away, but they catch me by the collar. "How could you, how could you, how could you?" they chant. "Your very own mother! Your very own us!" I'll stop writing. I'm sorry. And I do. I stop forever, and instantly my lips and hands are dotted with mold. White threads spread across my face where mushrooms begin to swell. I grow wild with silence.

"Oh, for god's sake," says my mother. "Forget it. Enough with the drama."

"But my silence is real," wrote the twentieth-century French philosopher Maurice Blanchot. "If I hid it from you, you would find it again a little farther on."

Of all the silences in fairy tales, the most pronounced is the Little Mermaid's. For a potion that will turn her into a human, she pays the sea witch with her voice. In Hans Christian Andersen's "The Little Mermaid," the sea witch lives where no flowers or sea grass grow, where "all the trees and bushes were polyps, half animals and half plants." It's the sea witch's silence, her exile, her house built from the bones of shipwrecked humans, the toad feeding out of her mouth, and the snakes sprawled like illegible cursive "about her great spongy bosom" that is the silence of poets. It's Blanchot's silence. It's the silence of outsiders and mothers. Once kept it will run ahead and wait for all of us to catch up. And as it waits, it will grow.

The Little Mermaid's silence is the silence of children. But the sea witch's silence is the silence of an old woman with a story no one will ever know. The first silence is soft and lovesick and melancholy like sea foam. The second silence surrounds you as water surrounds a drowning woman, transparent and cruel.

It's been a difficult year. My stepdaughter moved in for seven months and then moved out. She left Mavis, her pet tarantula, behind. My husband and I argued more than ever. My grandmother died so I couldn't call her up to ask her advice. In an act of grief, I bought a yellow rotary telephone for my desk. It's plugged into nothing. Sometimes I just hold the receiver up to my ear and listen. Sometimes I talk.

As the date of my stepdaughter's departure grew closer, I practiced politely biting my tongue. There was so much to say, but I said nothing. I bit and I bit. "Peace," I once wrote in a story about daughters, "is what pain looks like in public."

As Blanchot promised, my silence returned "a little farther on." A tree began to grow right in the middle of my house. Instead of seeds, its fruit had sharp little needles. I don't know what this fruit is called, but it's no fruit you want. I pushed my thumbs inside and split the flesh. I rinsed the pulp off a sticky needle and threaded it. In my own house, I said nothing and then more nothing, and the tree thickened. And now it's winter, and my house has grown a tree, and this tree bears fruit, and with its needle-seeds I begin to sew. I make a sewing. It's not a dress. Or a shawl. There is nowhere for a body to go inside this sewing. It's a long and narrow thing. It's the cold path home if the rest of the fairy tale were missing.

"Hi." I show the sewing to Mavis the tarantula, because I probably shouldn't show it to my husband, and my grandmother is dead, and my stepdaughter has gone back to her mother's, and my sons should be spared, and also it's imaginary. Mavis is crouched over a live cricket struggling in her web. Mavis is too busy with her own silence to look up. And even if she did look up, she'd probably just blame me for having been left behind.

I can hardly bear to look at Mavis, and yet I can't stop looking. "Good morning, Mavis. You okay?"

"I don't want to hear one word about that tarantula," says my mother. "Not one word."

"I felt it shelter," wrote Emily Dickinson, "to speak to you."

"Oh my god, Sabrina," says a dear friend, "set the fucking thing free."

I feel for the sea witch. To whom can she talk other than the bottom of the sea? On the flight back from my brother's home after Thanksgiving, I watch the 1989 Disney animated feature *The Little Mermaid*. It's lousy with ideological traps. It's empty of what makes Hans Christian Andersen's fairy tales so dark and alluring. No lavish agony disguised as piety. No cultish suffering. In Disney it's all big, bright eyes, high hopes, and too much singing. The sea witch has a name: Ursula, which means "little bear," even though she seems to be an octopus. She wears a gold nautilus around her neck, and this is where she keeps Ariel's voice after Ariel signs her voice away with a fishbone. That the sea witch had once ruled the kingdom has been added to the fairy tale. But why she's been banished remains untold even though she's marked all over by her banishment.

Eli watches with me but grows bored and plays a word game instead. There is rough air. My water slides off the tray and spills. Eli keeps asking me to help him unscramble letters to make words, but the plane is shuddering through clouds, and I'm holding his hand too tightly. "Mama! We'll either die or we won't die. Just tell me one word." And I do. It's *stop*.

A student asks me if I ever wonder if I should just stop writing. "Is it really worth it?" she asks. "All this

vulnerability? All this exposure? Possibly hurting everyone you love?"

I tell her language is what I have, and I think without
it I'd grow tentacles, and sharp little teeth would poke
through my skull. She laughs. "I'm serious," I say. "If I
stopped writing, I'd go sea witch."

"But shouldn't certain things be left sacred?" she
asks. "Like your children?"

The word *children* floats above my head like a magnificent cloud about to burst. And when it bursts, I will
be drenched by them. All day I am drenched by them. A
holy water. Why, I wonder, should the sacred be unsay-
able? How can I write about motherhood without writing about my children? Who would play their part? The
birds in the trees? A stranger? The shadows?

"Why," asks my stepdaughter, "did you write about
me?" Another cloud. I look up. It's in the shape of a
heart, no, a mouth.

I want to say something about repair. About fixing
us. About love, and fear, and hard work. About wanting
to help her. But instead I say, "This is my life, too." And
the cloud thins.

The nautilus shell Ursula wears around her neck is
hollow. The shell is a living fossil, like a fairy tale. Like a
fairy tale, it's an ancient casing that once held a breathing thing in place. A similar spiral is encrypted in the
inner ear and hurricanes and spiderwebs and the uterus.
It is proof of where a story once lived or tried to live,
and it's marked by the same elliptical orbit that makes it

practically impossible to tell where one thing begins and where it ends.

"It is true," writes the poet Lucie Brock-Broido, "that each self keeps a secret self which cannot speak when spoken to." I've been teaching my secret self to speak. It bleats hungrily. Its legs are spindly, and its heart is ancient. It was my husband who once helped me build it a room with stained-glass windows and a bed for waking up and dreaming.

Many years ago, when I was around my stepdaughter's age, I burned my arms with cigarettes. I can still count on my arm how many times I did it: twelve. A collection of full white moons. A lit-up path down my left arm that hasn't faded. I was twenty, and I loved someone who was cruel. I became silent and gaunt and wrote little down. And so the answer I gave to my student is wrong. If I stopped writing, I'd be covered in moons. Their light would be so blinding I'd barely be able to see my children. Or my mother standing at my front door crying.

"When I was little," says Eli, "I thought the moon was following me."

"Me, too," I say.

In 1978, two young scientists studying 500-million-year-old nautilus shells discovered that the number of lines on each chamber was consistent with the time it takes for the moon to revolve around the earth. Today's shells have thirty lines on each chamber, but shells from 420 million years ago have only nine lines per chamber.

Which means the moon once revolved around the earth in nine days. Which means the moon was once closer. Which means silence was once closer, too. We hide and hide our silences. And yet like the moon, they're still here. They're just a little farther on.

14

Bah, Humbug

It is December in Georgia, and we are driving past twinkling lights, and wreaths, and mildly poisonous winterberries, and a wire reindeer whose red nose softly glows on and off, on and off. Eli looks out the window.

"Can we have a Christmas tree, Mama?"

"No."

Silence.

"What if we paint it black?"

I consider this.

The holiday season does not bring out the best in me. I go sour and frantic. Mandatory cheer sinks my spirit. For my sons, I pile up presents for the eight days of Chanukah. The house grows small and dizzy as toys and more toys are torn from their boxes. The menorahs flicker, and yes, they're beautiful, but if there is a miracle here, who could find it under all this pleasure? "It is possible I am doing everything wrong." I say this to my husband three times a day, like I'm praying, until December is over.

I'm awful at holidays, I know. Years ago, watching the Thanksgiving Day Parade in Manhattan, I was so nervous my whole family would fall off the roof that I was told to sit in the stairwell because I was ruining it for everybody. Where's my December stairwell? I'll go sit in it until everybody, after the new year, comes back down.

E.T.A. Hoffmann's 1817 "The Nutcracker and the Mouse King" opens with Marie and Fritz "huddled together in a corner of a little back room." They hear a "distant hammering," and shuffling and murmuring, and Fritz tells his sister a small dark man has crept down the hallway with a big box under his arm. The small man is Drosselmeier. The children call him their god-papa. He wears a black eye patch, and a wig made from strands of glass. He is as much toy as toymaker. "You're just like my old Jumping Jack," says Marie, "that I threw away last month." *Dross* is waste, and *drosseln* in German is to "stir things up." And Drosselmeier is both. He is December. He is the month that makes waste insepa-rable from delight.

Drosseln also means "to choke." And it also means "a thrush," a speckled songbird. The bird that sounds like a flute in the woods. Over and over again, Drossel-meier is exactly what he isn't.

Around the time I was trying to get pregnant, and my stepdaughter was eight, my husband bought her two goldfish. Over the years, although my husband spent hours cleaning it, the tank darkened and smelled like old garlic, but the fish thrived. One of the fish (I don't remember if she had a name) was always pregnant, or having babies, or eating her babies. This is how December makes me feel. Like I am the most unpregnant person on earth watching a goldfish that is endlessly fertile eat her babies. "I am nothing, but I must be everything," wrote Karl Marx in *Contribution to the Critique of Hegel's Philosophy of Right,* imagining the utterance that precedes a revolution.

The holiday season, like a fairy tale, is for breeding the myths we consume, which will nourish us so that we can breed more myths to consume. An elliptical feast! A banquet of myths! We nibble our tales until we get to our head. By the end of December, we are full of ourselves. We are swollen with myth. And then on January 1, we make a resolution to be somehow different than how we are. We clean off our desks, thin out our air, and start again.

I don't buy my sons a Christmas tree and paint it black, but my mother and I do take them to the *Nutcracker* ballet, where she buys them each their own wooden nutcracker. Eli clicks the mouth open and shut, open and shut, open and shut, and is shushed. The Balanchine interpretation has the muscle of Hoffmann's story but not its bite. The astronomer is missing. Marie is now Clare. There is no Princess Pirlipat, and the horror of the mice has been softened into a joke involving a cannon that shoots cheese.

Eli is wearing his pajamas, and at intermission I hear

at least four audience members comment on this. "Is *that* boy in his *pajamas*?" I want to remind them that we're all in a nightmare disguised as a dream. That we're all fast asleep. That it's way past our bedtime. But I say nothing instead.

At the end of the ballet, the Cavalier almost doesn't catch the Sugarplum Fairy, and her fury brightens the stage like fake snow.

Like most fairy tales, "The Nutcracker and the Mouse King" is all hole and shell. If there is a kernel, it's already inside us. There are cracks everywhere: the ones in the kitchen for the mice to come through, the Nutcracker's broken teeth, Marie's cut arm, the bites in the sugar figures, the cracks that let fiction leak into reality, the toys running free through shattered glass, and a mother who disbelieves everything her daughter feels.

There is even an extra hole in the toymaker's face. I imagine a ballerina peeling back Drosselmeier's eye patch and climbing into the abyss in his head. I'd follow her. All the way down the socket. Maybe that's where we'll spend next December. Inside Drosselmeier. Not where the toys are, but where they begin. A forest of rattles before they are shaken. The stirrings of a doll before her mouth is sewn on. A miniature airplane before its first soar. A four-day, five-night family vacation at the precipice of a man's imagination.

"And then you wonder," says my mother, "why Noah is so sensitive."

"What do you mean?" I say.

But I know what she means. She means my heart is contagious, and my eight-year-old son might be catching what I have. All winter, living with Noah has been a little like living with Werner Herzog. *What would happen if there was no wind? Where do we go when we no longer exist? Did you hear that sound? What if love is a person we don't know? What would happen if I had no DNA? Can you die from spilling milk on a mushroom?* Each question arrives like a pirouette balanced at the edge of a stage that only Noah can see. Each question is the dance of one thousand wise sons.

"To be radical," wrote Karl Marx, "is to grasp things by the root." Noah has a fistful of roots. A stunning bouquet. I sniff them, and these questions, to be honest, flood me with relief. It's when I don't know where the roots are, that's when I'm sullen.

None of Noah's questions comes with a toy. A toy is an answer to a question a child hasn't learned how to ask.

"My favorite part of the ballet," says my mother, "is Mother Ginger." Mother Ginger's giant crinoline skirt is a house filled with children. The door opens, and out they run. The tallest male ballerina plays this birth scene, forward and backward. At the end of the dance, he rewinds the children back into his body, which is also a house and a joke and a spectacle and a garment. Attached to Mother Ginger is a parasol, a fan, a mirror, and a tambourine. She is well stocked, but she can only move sideways. The trick is not to step on the children. The trick is for the children to never grow old.

My mother says Mother Ginger is her favorite part, but it's not really her favorite part. Her real favorite part is when the Sugar Plum Fairy almost falls and smacks the Cavalier in the face. "I like when things go awry," says my mother. She likes seeing the roots, too.

"Where's your holiday spirit?" asks a friend.

"It's hiding," I say. "It won't come out until yours goes back inside."

I don't know what's bothering me. Maybe it's that I spend a lot of time picking up broken toys, and so it's impossible to see piles of beautifully wrapped gifts without seeing the shred and the shard. Without seeing the albatross's belly turned vibrant from the plastics it picks from the ocean. A belly as colorful as a toy shop, and as dead. "Remember," says my husband, "when there was only one Superman?" And I do. I remember when there wasn't even one. I remember when all there was, at first, was biodegradable me. What if all a toy really is is just the absence of a mother? This morning I reached into my pocket for my house key, and found a small blue plastic leg instead. Every day I am reminded that ending up where you actually belong might be the biggest miracle of all.

When I was a little kid, I spent every Shabbat at my great-aunt's house. After lunch, our whole family would sit around the dining room table talking and singing and arguing and cracking open walnuts. The nutcracker didn't have a face. It was just a pair of long silver legs as strong as a ballerina's. I cracked open nut after nut and studied their wrinkles and folds. The two hemispheres looked exactly like the brain, which delighted me. I would eat too many and feel a little sick and happy. By late afternoon, the plastic tablecloth would be covered with shells and fading winter light. I want so badly to bring my sons to this table, but no one is sitting there anymore. As each December cracks open and leaves only its shell behind, I want to give something to my sons to hold. Something like belonging. Something that will last. But I don't know what. All I have is this kernel. And it's too small to see.

15

Fairy Tales and the Bodies of Black Boys

Noah and I go to Target. He is carrying a little stuffed monkey, and as we walk through the automatic doors, he puts it under his shirt. "No, no," I say.

"Bondo is shy," he says. "I told him I'd keep him safe."

"No, no," I say. Under Noah's shirt, Bondo could be anything. He could be wild and alive. He could be something that doesn't belong to him. He could be a bouquet of flowers or a gun or a book of fairy tales about the bodies of Black boys.

"Why?" he asks.

"Why—" I answer, or I start saying something and then stop, or I say "Because it isn't safe," or I say "I love you," or I say "Here, let me hold him."

A few days later, a friend posts on Facebook that her nine-year-old Black son is now riding his bike to the supermarket by himself. "We have talked to him," she writes, "about using a bag for the items he's bought, not his pockets, keeping his receipt in his hand as he leaves the store, keeping his hands out of his pockets while shopping, taking his hood off." I imagine it continuing, "We have given him invisibility powder, we have made wings for him out of the feathers of ancient doves, we have given him the power to become a rain cloud and burst, if necessary, into a storm."

When I was a child, I could've hidden a house under my dress, and all I would've been was a girl with a house under her dress.

As my sons grow, the American imagination grows around them like water hemlock. Poisonous and hollow. My sons' skin is light. So the hemlock may not grow as thick as it would for a darker boy.

I look for a fairy tale about the bodies of boys. There is Pinocchio, but he's wooden. And Peter Pan, although magical, is only the thin memory of a boy. There is Jack and his beanstalk, but Jack is more wish than body. And then I remember Tom Thumb who, like the body of the Black boy, is caught inside a swallow cycle.

The History of Tom Thumb, published in 1621, was the first fairy tale printed in English. A metrical version was published in 1630. A plowman and his wife long for a child, but no child comes until Merlin, the magician, grants them a son no bigger than the father's thumb: "that men should heare him speake, but not / his wan-dring shadow touch." Tom Thumb is conceived and born in half an hour. The fairies visit him and make him a hat from an oak leaf, a shirt from a spider's web, boots from mouse skin, socks from apple peels, and a belt from his mother's eyelash.

Tom Thumb is swallowed over and over again. He is swallowed by a red cow, a raven, a giant, a fish, a frog, a cinched sack filled with cherry pits, a mousetrap, and King Arthur's court (because his "merry tricks pleased the queen"). Will my sons, as they grow, become more and more vulnerable to ravishment? Will they be eaten and spat out? Will they be sent into a swallow cycle to satisfy the hunger of our dear, sick country?

I don't want my sons anywhere near the mouth of this country. I am the mother looking up and calling, *Get down from there*. They pretend not to hear me. They are so happy and free.

With twine, Tom Thumb's mother ties him to a this-tle while she milks the cows so the wind doesn't carry him off.

I am the mother who is trying to untie my sons from a fairy tale that doesn't exist. A fairy tale that could carry them away. It's the one about a war that's being fought by children. But the children don't even know there is a war, and the children think they're still chil-dren. This fairy tale doesn't exist because it isn't a fairy tale. It's right outside. Put your hand through your kitchen window. Can you feel it?

"The wind of my life," wrote James Baldwin, "was blowing me away."

Many years ago I wrote a poem that began, "A few

days before the first snow the soldiers dressed like children began to appear." It ends with all the soldier children sailing away to another land. Where is our sailboat? Where is the sea? How far is the land?

"What's your plan for middle school?" asks a mother. "Where is our sailboat? How far is the most faraway land?"

At four a.m. Eli comes into my bed. He smells like freshly baked bread and wet twigs. "I had a dream," he says. "I went into another dimension where there were no letters or numbers. Only signs."

"Signs?" I ask.

"Like this one," he says. He points his index fingers down. It looks like an upside-down peace sign. Or the tiny legs of a tiny boy walking away.

"What's your plan for middle school?" asks a mother. *We are looking into,* I want to say, *other dimensions.*

When it rains, Tom Thumb sleeps in a buttonhole. He crawls through keyholes and sails away in an eggshell. He dances a minuet on the queen's fingernail. His body is the magic that will conquer him. His smallness is a spell cast over his body that is his beginning, his middle, and his end.

In one version of Tom Thumb, he dies by the breath of a poisonous spider. In another, a woman coughs on him. At the end, what is most dangerous is not the swallow but the breath that lives inside it. Like a slur crawling over the lip and hitting the air.

I ask my husband what he would have said to Noah.

"I would've let him keep Bondo under his shirt."

"And then what?" I ask.

"And then nothing," he says, "because God help anyone who tried to mess with him."

Sometimes I wonder if my husband slips through little rips in space and time. He is always as much here as he is not here. Like dusk if dusk were a man. Maybe this is how he has outwitted the swallow. Maybe this is what he prays resides in our sons. Maybe he, too, is planning a move to another dimension.

When I was pregnant with Eli, the sonographer had me return three times because each time she waved the wand over my belly, Eli would cover his face, which cast a dark shadow over his heart. "It's nothing," said the sonographer. "It's just hard to see his heart through the shadow."

By writing this down, am I swallowing my children and their father, too? By naming them, do I swallow them? By being afraid, do I swallow them? Sometimes I just want to hide them all under my coat. And walk through a world where nothing is ever named Target.

I wonder if somewhere there's a very, very old fairy tale that dried, hardened, and eventually cracked. I imagine I might find it one day, and when I do, something alive will stumble out and whisper into my ear all the answers to all the questions my sons will ever ask me about fear and hate.

This morning Noah asked me to help him tighten the belt on his pants. "I must be shrinking!" he said. "I'm the incredible shrinking man!"

But he isn't shrinking. He is growing. May my sons live, like Tom Thumb, to be one hundred and one. May the wind never carry them away.

16

Sleeping with the Wizard

When I was nineteen, I lived with a wizard. Her hair was like dandelion seed, and she had a map of a faded country crookedly taped to her bedroom wall. She smoked unfiltered Lucky Strikes, and her clothes were always wrinkled, and she gave me Walter Benjamin and the poems of Paul Celan, and she kept me secret. No one knew I lived with a wizard in an awful, cold apartment that cost $940 a month. She spoke many languages in an accent that seemed to originate from an ancient ruin. I thought she might give me a brain. I already had a dumb heart and even dumber courage. She was the farthest place from home I could go. The first time we kissed, I knew she would undo me.

In L. Frank Baum's *The Wonderful Wizard of Oz,* the Great Oz appears as a head, a lady dressed in "green silk gauze," a beast, and a ball of fire. The first time my wizard appeared to me, she was my literature professor. Her office had no window. I don't remember her ever smiling, though she did laugh, and so her laugh must have resided in a face slightly distant from her face. Like two cities over. I didn't know then, as I know now, the difference between worship and love.

The Wizard in Baum is a humbug. He's a sweetheart and a fake. My wizard was no sweetheart, and she was no fake. She needed no curtain because I was the curtain. When I pulled myself all the way back, there she was. The Wizard of Oz's real name was nine men long: Oscar Zoroaster Phadrig Isaac Norman Henkle Emmannuel Ambroise Diggs. My wizard's real name was a little girl's name. It was the wrong name for her. Her name was the name of a drawing of a girl eating an ice cream cone in a soft pink dress. But I called her by her name anyway. And she called me by mine.

What even is a wizard? A master, a father, a mother, a lover, a god, a magician, a rabbi, a priest, a president, a beautiful, enraged professor? Like Godot, the wizard can be a holding place for what we emit but can't yet claim or name or know. Our dust in the sunlight. The spell we have but don't yet know how to cast. Each of us wants something different from the wizard. I wanted to be undone.

"On the fabrication of the Master," writes the poet Lucie Brock-Broido, "he began as a Fixed star."

Unlike the Scarecrow's brains and the Tin Man's heart and the Lion's courage, Dorothy Gale's home wasn't already inside her. She had a strong wind. It was already in her name. It was a twister. By lifting her up and whirling her around, it saves her from "growing as gray as her other surroundings." It gives her life. "She felt," wrote Baum, "as if she were being rocked gently, like a baby in a cradle."

The wizard was my twister. But I didn't touch down in Munchkin Land. I wasn't welcomed as "a noble Sorceress." I landed only a few miles from where I grew up. I landed in a cold apartment filled with German philosophy and cigarette ash, where my wizard would eventually—on a sunless day—call me a parasite. A horsehair worm. A barnacle. A sponge. My wizard meant she was my host. She meant I was eating her.

When I left the wizard, I weighed eighty-eight pounds. I was as heavy as two infinities.

I left the wizard and went to my mother.

I don't remember my mother saying a single word. She just opened the door and let me in. I had my cat Lucy with me. We were back from Oz.

There's no place like home when there's nowhere else to go.

This is not a cautionary tale about falling in love with your professor. It's not that simple, and anyway, years later, when I was a grown-up, I married one, and our love is tender and complicated and true. My story, like everybody's story, is a question with at least two opposing answers. Just like there are good witches and bad witches, there are wizards who give us doors that lead into rooms filled with light and love and there are wizards who give us doors that lead into rooms filled with booby traps and dust.

"Over a period of a year," writes Brock-Broido, "then another, then more years, my idea of the Master began an uprush—he became a kind of vortex of tempests & temperaments, visages and voicelessness. He took on the fractured countenance of a composite portrait, police-artist sketch. Editor, mentor, my aloof proportion, the father, the critic, beloved, the wizard—he was beside himself."

When I was nineteen, a wizard kissed me and gave me a pit I thought was a seed, but it wasn't a seed. It was a hole. And down, down, down I fell.

The wizard and I spent many hours in bed watching Holocaust documentaries. She took me to Rome to meet her father, whom she hated. Afterward we drove to Amsterdam, where she gave a paper on the superego at the fifth conference of the International Society of European Ideas, and then she ignored me for days. I saw nothing of Amsterdam but the inside of her rage—which, like a tornado, was the color of a bruise in the sky. Black and blue with spots of yellow.

"I think you are a very bad man," Dorothy tells the Wizard.

"Oh, no, my dear; I'm really a very good man," he replies, "but I'm a very bad Wizard, I must admit."

Each time my wizard appeared to me, her face was a different face. She spun like a slot machine. Her face was three reels. Sometimes it stopped on disgust, love, and despair all at once. I had no lever, and I had no coins. I never won.

It's not that my wizard was a terrible wizard, it was just that she was a very bad man.

Listen, it must hurt to be a wizard. For hours my wizard would lock herself in her study and write about hypnosis, and trauma, and empathy, and fascination, and catastrophe, and survival, and anxiety, and disarray, and freedom. It sounded like hail. It smelled like smoke. I sat in the living room and played solitaire. When she emerged, she emerged like the Wizard arriving to Oz: "But I found myself in the midst of a strange people who, seeing me come from the clouds, thought I was a great Wizard. Of course I let them think so, because they were afraid of me, and promised to do anything I wished them to."

On my twenty-first birthday, we drove to Montauk, the easternmost point of New York State, also known as "The End." She gave me no card or gift or even a spoken "happy birthday." We took a road called 495 as far as it went, and then there we were. Did I even look at the ocean? I didn't. Did I make a wish? I don't think so. Why did I love her? I cannot remember.

Why am I writing this down? If my sons, when they are older, ever read this, I will say this is just a tornado in the shape of a chapter. This is just a very bad dream.

I've carried my wizard around with me for twenty-five years, like a brick. A yellow brick that could be mistaken, when the sunlight hits it wrong, for fool's gold.

In the 1939 classic film *The Wizard of Oz*, the tornado was actually a muslin stocking spun around in dust and dirt. The snow in the poppy scene was made of asbestos, and the flying monkeys were only six inches high, cast out of rubber, and hung by piano wire. I believe in the necessity of illusion. Without it, the boy in bed looking out his window who sees the tree branches against the night sky as long, skinny men will blink the branch back into view before the men even have a chance to sing. Without illusion there is no metaphor. And without metaphor there is no poetry. When I looked at the wizard's face and heard the words she spoke, none I can now remember, I shook with gratitude. She chose me, and not you, or you, or you, to bear raw witness to her genius.

One of the last images I have of my wizard is her dandelion-seed head yelling out the window, like a furious flower, as I walked quickly away forever. I have zero memory of what she was yelling. I wish it had been the call of a wizard crying out for her hot air balloon to come carry her away, but I know it wasn't. It must have been November, but I remember it as a night in June.

It wasn't raining, or maybe it was. Maybe I was melting. Maybe my wizard was writing "Surrender Sabrina" with the smoke from her Lucky Strike in the night sky. All I know is that it was a night of two broken hearts, and everything was all mixed up. Look at all these pieces. It's impossible to tell who was the witch, who was the wizard, and who was the girl.

I would like to say I wrote myself away from the wizard. I would like to say every word I wrote was another yellow brick I lifted up and left behind. But that's not true. The road I walk is a spiral. And there's a heap of bricks in the middle. I once looked out, and my sons were climbing it. This is a true story. Their knees were scraped and their cheeks were flushed. When they got to the top, they asked, "Will we learn a lesson?"

"Like what?" I asked.

"Like what happens when you do something dangerous," they said.

I wanted to say *Come down*, but instead I said, "Sometimes you fall, but sometimes you get to see something you otherwise wouldn't have seen."

"And what good is that?" asked my sons.

I gave them an answer. It was a perfect answer. But by then they were so high up they could no longer hear a word I said.

17

The Fairy-Tale Virus

Once upon a time a Virus with a Crown on Its Head swept across the land. An invisible reign. A new government. "Go into your homes," said the Virus, "or I will eat your lungs for my breakfast, lunch, and dinner. The city that never sleeps shall fall into a profound slumber, your gold shall turn to dust, and your face shall be pressed against the windowpane.

"And the elders, for fear of death, shall not embrace the young."

The Virus was colorless and cruel. Some believed it to be the child of a bat, but no one knew its origin for sure. Some said it reminded them of a dead gray sun.

The fairy tale I will write about is this one. The one we were once inside.

All night I dream of buying a chicken. I am scared of us all getting sick, so I need to make jars and jars of bone broth to freeze, but there are no chickens left in the poultry section of our supermarket. Instead, just cold, empty shelves. They glow white like hospital beds. If I can't find a chicken, I should at least sew my sons' birth certificates into their woolen coats, but it's springtime, and pink dogwood is blooming everywhere, and where are we going? We are going nowhere.

I don't know when I'll be able to see my mother again.

"What day is it?" asks Noah. He wanders away before I can even answer.

It is almost Passover, which, like a fairy tale and a virus, depends on repetition. Every year, on the fifteenth of Nisan, we retell the story of the exodus from Egypt. We dip our pinkies into a full glass of red wine, and for every plague brought upon the Egyptians we make a stain: one for blood, one for frogs, one for lice, one for a maelstrom of beasts, one for pestilence, one for boils, one for hail, one for locusts, one for darkness, and one for the killing of the firstborn. For $14.99 on Amazon, you can buy a bag of plagues that includes plastic frogs and insects, white balls for hail, a sticky hand with white dots for boils, red ink for blood, a plush cow, and a finger puppet of a dead boy. "Delight the kids," reads the advertisement, "with a bag of plagues. Fun and educational." I think we'll skip the plagues this year.

A friend of mine texts me that her neighbor wants to know what our plans are for Passover. *"Tell her we're already inside it,"* I write. *"Tell her we don't need to celebrate it. It's celebrating us."*

She writes back, *"I'm telling her I'm putting blood on my gate and waiting for death to pass over my house."*

"*Even better,*" I write.

This is the problem with metaphor and ritual and fairy tales. Sometimes they start leaking into reality, and no one knows how to sew up the tear. And even if we did know how to sew it up, all the stores are out of needle and thread.

For a story to live, it must attach, enter, replicate, biosynthesize, assemble, and release. Fairy tales, like a virus that blooms into a global pandemic, cross borders and enter us. The storyteller is the infector. The storyteller retells their body's story in the body of another.

I keep thinking about the bat, the rumored mother of this Virus with a Crown on Its Head. I wonder what her fur smelled like, and what it felt like when she wrapped her wings around her thin body like a cloak. Did she swoop? Was she frightened? Was her tongue long? What must it be like, I wonder, to be the bat that started this cavalcade of coughing that shook an entire planet. But then I remember that every story begins with a bat. If not for your mother there would be no you. So your mother is a bat, and my mother is a bat. I am a bat. You are a bat. My sons are bats. Every action we've ever taken is a bat. Every wildflower we ever picked is a bat. Sex is a bat, and the soup you'll eat tonight is a bat. This virus is a bat, and its cure is a bat. Poems, even their crossed-out lines, are bats. Our lungs are bats. Death is a bat, and birth is a bat. The moon, the sun, and the stars in the sky are all bats. And when you cannot sleep at night, that too is a bat. And when you are afraid, your fear is a bat. And God, who created all the bats, is also a bat. And not believing in God is a bat, too.

I listen to my old rabbi on Zoom speak about lessons in times of crisis. He looks tired, and his eye twitches.

On the eleventh day of sheltering in place, Noah tells me he had a dream he was drawing and his drawings were drawing drawings and those drawings were drawing, too. My son understands what we reap is what we sow, that what we bat is what we bat. Maybe that is the moral of this unending fairy tale. Maybe the moral is that what's outside us is what's inside us, too.

"What's your favorite day of the coronavirus so far?" asks Eli. His happiness might be the best bat of all.

This Passover our exodus will be made not by wandering a desert but by a desert—a desertion—wandering through us. *Do not feel lonely,* says the Virus with a Crown on Its Head, *the entire universe is inside you.* The Virus is quoting Rumi, who meant this as a blessing, but the Virus means it as a curse.

The reason why fairy tales exist and thrive is because our bodies recognize them like they are our own. Our same blood type. Because we recognize *wolf, witch, forest, kiss, curse, spell,* and *mother,* the stories latch. If the image blurs as it crosses cultural borders, its latch will thin and possibly vanish. Each spike on the Virus's crown is like a key that unlocks a cell. Each image in a fairy tale is like a key that opens us up, too. We are its host. The virus and the fairy tale leave little messages inside our cells to replicate. What the Virus whispered to the bat is the same story the Virus is whispering to us. It's a message that brings us closer to each other than we've ever been.

On our honeymoon, my husband bought me a plague doctor. I saw him gazing out a frosted shop window in Barcelona on a street that today, I'm certain, is completely deserted. He stood twelve inches tall. He looked me dead in the eye, like a warning from the past, and I wanted him immediately. He wore a ruffled collar, a long brown cape, and a porcelain beak that in the seventeenth century would've been filled with juniper berries, roses, mint leaves, camphor, cloves, and myrrh.

If I remember right, the doctor cost only sixty-two dollars, which seemed like a bargain. I was pregnant with Noah at the time and glowing with hope. As it turns out, plague doctors rarely cured their patients. Instead, they served to make a public record of the infected and the dead. They could not heal, only witness. To the dying, they must have appeared nightmarish: half doctor, half animal. Their long beaks heavy with medicine and herbs they'd never dispense, only inhale. The sticks they carried were used not to fix but to keep a distance. Why did I want the plague doctor? I am not sure. Maybe I wanted him because he reminded me of me, writing down things that are happening or have happened.

18

Fuck the Bread, the Bread Is Over

In February, as a plague enters America, I am a finalist for a job I am not offered.

I am brought to campus for a three-day interview. I am shown the library I'll never have access to, and introduced to students I'll never teach. I shake hands with faculty I'll never see again. I describe in great detail the course on fairy tales I'll never offer. I stand up straight in a simple black-and-white dress.

"Don't say anything strange," said my mother. "Don't blather," she said. "You have a tendency to blather."

I meet with a dean who rubs his face until it reddens, then asks me whether writers even belong in universities. I meet with another dean who asks me the same thing. There are so many deans. I cannot tell the deans apart. Another dean asks me who the babies in my first collection of poems, *The Babies,* actually are. "We only have a few minutes left," he adds.

"They don't exist," I think I say. I'm hurrying. "I was writing about voices we'll never hear," I think I say.

He stands up and shakes my hand. I shake so many hands. I can't tell if everything is at stake or nothing is at stake. All I know is that I am being tested, and whether I am offered this job will depend on the appetite and mood of strangers.

Your final task, I imagine the dean saying, *is to make a rope out of these ashes. Do it and the job is yours.*

On the third day of the interview, the head of the creative writing department asks me if the courses I would be expected to teach should even exist.

"No," I wish I had said as I made my body gently vanish. "They shouldn't exist at all." Instead I say yes and pull a beautiful, made-up reason from the air and offer it to him as a gift. *Gold for your dust, sir. Pearls for your pigs.*

"Who is watching your sons right now?" he asks.

"Their father," I answer.

What does it mean to be worth something? Or worth enough? Or worthless? What does it mean to earn a living? What does it mean to be hired? What does it mean to be let go?

It's May now. More than thirty million Americans have lost their jobs. What mattered in February hardly seems to matter now. My sons, my husband, and I are lucky. We have stayed healthy, and we have enough money and enough food to eat. In between teaching my sons the difference between a scalene triangle and an isosceles, and moving my writing workshops from my garage to pixelated classrooms, and cleaning my house, and going nowhere, and being scared, and looking for bread flour and yeast, I can barely remember what it felt like to plead my case for three straight days. It feels good to barely remember.

"You write a lot about motherhood," says the sixteenth or seventeenth dean.

In the Grimms' "Cherry," an old king with three sons cannot decide who of the three should inherit the kingdom, and so he gives his sons three trials. In the first, they should seek "cloth so fine" the king can draw it through his golden ring. In the second, they are to find a dog small enough to fit inside a walnut shell. And in the third, they are to bring home the "fairest lady" in all the land. In the Grimms' "The Six Servants," a prince will win his princess if he brings back a ring the old queen has dropped into the Red Sea, devour three hundred oxen ("skin and bones, hair and horns"), drink three hundred barrels of wine, and keep his arms around the princess all night without falling asleep. And in "Rumpelstiltskin," if the poor miller's daughter spins larger and larger rooms full of straw into gold, she will become queen. If not, she will die. Fairy tales are riddled with tasks like these. Some contenders cheat, and some were never worthy, and some take the dreary, barren road, and some take the smooth, shady one, and some are helped by birds, and some are helped by giants, and some by witches, and some by luck.

I call my mother. "I can't find bread flour or yeast anywhere."

"Fuck the bread," she says. "The bread is over."

In fairy tales, form is your function, and function is your form. If you don't spin the straw into gold or inherit the kingdom or devour all the oxen or find the flour or get the professorship, you drop out of the fairy tale and fall over its edge into an endless blank forest where there is no other function for you, no alternative career. The future for the sons who don't inherit the kingdom is vanishment. What happens when your skills are no longer needed for the sake of the fairy tale? A great gust comes and carries you away.

In fairy tales, the king is the king. If he is dethroned, his bones clatter into a heap and vanish. Loosen the seams of the stepmother and reach in. Nothing but stepmother inside. Even when the princess is cinders and ash, she is still entirely princess.

I send my sons on a scavenger hunt because it's day fifty-eight of homeschooling, and I'm all out of ideas. I give them a checklist: a rock, soil, a berry, something soft, a red leaf, a brown leaf, something alive, something dead, an example of erosion, something that looks happy, a dead branch on a living tree. They come back with two canvas totes filled with nature. I can't pinpoint what this lesson is exactly. Something about identification and possession. Something about buying time. As I empty the bags and touch the moss, and the leaves, and the twigs, and the berries, and a robin-blue eggshell, I consider how much we depend on useless, arbitrary tasks to prove ourselves. I consider how much we depend on these tasks so we can say, at the very end, we succeeded.

Tomorrow, on day fifty-nine, I will ask my sons to "find me an acre of land / Between the salt water and the sea-strand, / Plough it with a lamb's horn, / Sow it all over with one peppercorn, / Reap it with a sickle of leather, / And gather it up with a rope made of heather." I will tell them if they perform each of these tasks perfectly, they will be rewarded with more tasks. And if they perform each of those tasks perfectly, they will be rewarded with more. Until at last, they will not be able to tell the difference between their hands and another boy's hands.

Over the years, I have applied for hundreds of professorships and even received some interviews. I've wanted a job like this for so long, I barely even know why I want it anymore. I look at my hands. I can't tell if they're mine.

"Of course you can tell if your hands are yours," says my mother. "Don't be ridiculous."

"I have no real job," I say.

"Of course you have a real job," she says.

"I have no flour," I say.

"Fuck the bread," says my mother again. "The bread is over."

And maybe the bread, as I've always understood it, really is over. The new world order is rearranging itself on the planet and settling in. Our touchstone is changing color. Our criteria for earning a life, a living, are mutating like a virus that wants badly to stay alive.

I text a friend, *"I can't find bread flour."*

She lives in Iowa. *"I can see the wheat,"* she says, *"growing in the field from outside my window."*

I watch a video on how to harvest wheat. I can't believe I have no machete. I can't believe I spent so many hours begging universities to hire me, I forgot to learn how to separate the chaff from the wheat and gently grind.

If I had a machete, I would use it to cut the mice, and the princess, and the king, and the stepmother, and the castle, and the wolf, and the mother, and the sons, free from their function so they could disappear into their own form.

But also I wanted an office with a number. I wanted a university ID. I wanted access to a fancy library and benefits and students and colleagues and travel money. I wanted the whole stupid kingdom.

"And then what?" says my mother.

"And then nothing," I say as I jump off the very top of a fairy tale that has no place for me.

"You're better off," says my mother.

I look around. I've landed where I am.

I like it here. I feel like I'm in Gertrude Stein territory, where the buttons are so tender they've come undone. The whole kingdom is spilling out of itself. There are holes everywhere. To the east, a pile of impossible tasks of my own making. To the west, a mountain of broken crowns I will melt and recast into a machete. "This is so nice," wrote Gertrude Stein, "and sweet and yet there comes the change, there comes the time to press more air. This does not mean the same as disappearance."

It's day sixty of homeschooling. Eli asks me to remind him how to make an *aleph*. I take a pencil and draw it for him very carefully.

"It's like a branch," I say, "with two little twigs attached."

"You know what, Mama?" he says. "You'd make a really good teacher."

"Thank you," I say. And then I show him how to draw a *bet*.

19

I'm So Tired

I am writing about "Sleeping Beauty" when I get a text from my mother: *"It's lymphoma."* My sister. She is twenty. Three lumps on her neck. I erase everything I've written. And then I vomit.

Ever since we went into our homes and shut the door, I have been comforted by images of nature reclaiming deserted places. I search the Web and watch snow fall on a dead escalator in an abandoned mall. I find a tree growing out of a rotting piano. The pedals have disappeared into the earth, and on its brown wooden torso, someone has carved the initials *C+S* inside a heart. For hours, I search the Web for more. Goats walk through city streets as if remembering the woods that once grew there. White mushrooms push up through the floor of a cathedral. I trace each mushroom with my thumb. It makes me want to pray.

"I don't believe in anything anymore," says my mother.

"Don't say that," I say. "Please don't say that."

But she can't hear me. She's already somewhere far, far away.

Before the text from my mother, I had been writing about Charles Perrault's "The Sleeping Beauty in the Wood," because I wanted to write about the bramble. I wanted to write about the hedge of briars that grows around the castle when Sleeping Beauty pricks her finger on a spindle and falls asleep for one hundred years. I wanted to write about the fairy who touches the governesses, ladies-in-waiting, gentlemen, stewards, cooks, scullions, errand boys, guards, porters, pages, footmen, and the princess's little dog, Puff, so that they all fall asleep, too. I wanted to write about the kindness of the fairy who makes sure that when Beauty wakes up, she doesn't wake up alone. I wanted to write about the wind dying down, and the sleeping doves on the roof. I had an idea that the bramble was good. That what we've needed all along is for us to hold still and allow nature to grow wild around us. I had this idea that when we all woke up together, the bramble would teach us something. I imagined we'd all rub our eyes and a new civilization would hobble toward the bramble and learn to read its script. I imagined the bramble clasped together like hands filled with cures and spells. I imagined we'd learn a lesson that could save us.

"The lesson," says my mother, "is that we're all going to die." But my mother doesn't say this. She would've said this two weeks ago before my sister was diagnosed with lymphoma because it's like a thing my mother would say. But now when she speaks she sounds different. She has an echo now. Like the only mother awake in a castle filled with sleeping daughters.

My sister is breathtakingly beautiful. This is a fact. When she walks into a room, people turn around and stare.

"Maybe you should write about widows instead," says my husband. A small vine begins to creep up his neck and winds around his face.

"I am not writing about widows," I say. And the vine vanishes.

When I was twenty-nine and my sister was five, my mother and I brought her to Disneyland, where you can eat breakfast at Cinderella's castle with all the princesses. The princesses came out all at once, as if through a hole in the air, and spun around in their blue and pink and yellow gowns. My sister climbed onto the table and reached her arms out. Had my mother and I not pulled her back down, she would've let the princesses pick her up and carry her away.

I write about Sleeping Beauty, and then I erase everything I write about Sleeping Beauty, while my husband starts saving eggshells, and carrot peels, and coffee grounds, and bread, and dryer lint, and banana peels, and orange rinds in a plastic container that sits on our kitchen counter. He has started worm composting. In three to six months, he promises we will have nutrient-rich soil to grow more flowers and vegetables. I am worried there won't be enough airflow, and he will forget to harvest the worm castings, and all the worms will die. I am worried about maggots and rot.

"Trust me," he says. "Please trust me."

And he's right. I need to trust him more. And I need to trust the worms and the air and the soil more, too. But I'm still worried.

"I wish everyone would just fall asleep," says my mother, "and not wake up until Sasha is okay again."

I want to assure her when Sleeping Beauty wakes up, she gives birth to a son and a daughter named Day and Dawn. But what a stupid thing to say. What good am I? An old daughter writing about fairy tales when I should be cooking my mother and sister actual soup.

"She's going to lose all her hair," says my mother, which makes me want to cut off mine and swallow it.

"Your book came," says my husband. He hands me Christopher Payne's *North Brother Island.*

I had ordered it weeks ago, and had half given up on its ever arriving. It's a book of photographs of an uninhabited island of ruins in the middle of the East River. Once used as an overspill for college dormitories, then as a quarantine hospital island to treat infectious disease, and then later for drug addiction, it was abandoned in 1963. A forest of kudzu and rust grows around it. Sunlight bounces off disappearing buildings. Water drips through collapsing roofs. Oh, brotherless North Brother. Even the herons who made it a sanctuary flew away in 2011, and no one knows why. And then the swallows came.

"I can't find my goddamn earbuds," says my mother. I imagine peonies and daffodils and heliotrope blooming from her ears. "Let me call you back," she says.

But she doesn't call back. She forgets to call me back. My sister has lymphoma, and that's all any of us can remember. I imagine her phone crisscrossed by spiderwebs and dust.

In the pages I erased, I wrote about the old fairy. The one who was forgotten. The one who was assumed dead or bewitched, but she wasn't. She was very much alive, but when Beauty is born, she isn't invited to the ceremony. And so when the fairies bestow gifts upon the princess, the old fairy emerges from her dust and out of spite declares Beauty will die from a prick of the spindle. Another fairy steps out from behind a tapestry. She cannot undo the old fairy's spell, but she can change dying to sleep that will last a hundred years. In the pages I erase, I write something about how we are quarantined inside our kingdom because we forgot the old fairy. I write something about how we are not asleep, but we're also not awake. I write in the pages I erase that had I been the old fairy, I would've cursed us, too, and that we don't deserve to be kissed and woken up. But I take it all back. I want the bramble to part. When did this tear in a fairy tale become wide enough for my whole family to climb through? I want to beg the old fairy for forgiveness. Where is she? Who cursed my sister?

I want to go to North Brother Island, and just stand there until a patch of moss grows on my cheek. "I'm so tired," says my mother. "I'm so tired, I'm so tired, I'm so tired." I want to hold my mother's hand on North Brother Island. I don't remember ever holding my mother's hand though I must have, at least once, as a child. I want the moss to grow on my mother's cheek, too. When enough moss grows, I will peel it from our cheeks and boil it and give it to my sister on a spoon like medicine. Like a miracle cure.

I tell my mother about North Brother Island.

"Maybe we should buy it," she says. "I need somewhere to go."

What I don't tell my mother is that we have already gone somewhere. We are already in this place where the world we once knew is rushing out of us. We are standing in its unbearable greenness. There is a pinprick on my sister's finger that is so small and so black it can easily be mistaken for a pokeberry seed.

20

Rapunzel, Draft One Thousand

I call the Wig Man. He picks up. "My sister," I say, "was diagnosed—"

He interrupts me because he is driving, and he is in a rush. "My store," he says, "was looted last night."

My sister, I want to say. . . .

He tells me he gathered all the hair that was left on the floor. "Glass everywhere," he says. "I filled my Toyota Tacoma with all the hair that was left. I am driving home now. Is your sister's hair long?" he asks.

It is. It is very long.

"Because if it's long, what your sister should do before treatment begins is cut all her hair off, and I will sew it, strand by strand, into a soft net. It's called a halo," he says. "I want to help your sister," says the Wig Man.

I imagine his Toyota Tacoma so stuffed with wigs that black and brown and blond hairs press up against the windows. Like animals trapped inside their own freedom.

He starts to cry. I am certain he is driving across a bridge. "I don't know how much more of this I can take," he says.

"Neither do I," I don't say.

Sewing a wig strand by strand is called ventilating. With a needle you draw each strand through a lace net and knot it on itself. The needle goes in and then out like thousands of tiny breaths. Ventilating a wig takes the patience of the dead. Each knotted strand is like a person sewn into a free country. The knot is tight, and the net is manufactured.

"Of course my life matters," says Eli. "Why wouldn't it matter?"

My sister decides not to cut her hair. Instead she lets it fall out, slowly, then suddenly. She yawns, rises, and climbs up the stairs. She leaves behind a trail of blondish-gold thread, like a princess coming undone. I help my sister into bed, though she prefers I not touch her. On her nightstand are six glittering tiaras. She wears one to chemo. Another to breakfast.

"Isn't it strange," I say, "that I write about fairy tales, and you are a fairy-tale princess?"

She looks at me hard. "A sick princess," she says.

Of all the fairy tales, Rapunzel gives me the most difficult time. "It's because," says my husband, "you are trying to use her to write about systemic racism, and protest, and cancer, and a global pandemic."

"Should I just take out the racism?" I ask.

"No," he says. "You can't take out the racism."

"I know," I say. "That was a stupid question. Can I take out my mother?"

"Does your mother appear?" he asks. "I don't remember your mother appearing."

"Eventually," I say, "my mother always appears."

I am following my husband around the kitchen. "Should I add how after George Floyd was killed, you sat on the edge of the bathtub and cried? Remember how you said, 'We've been here before'? Remember when you said, 'When will this stop,' but you said it like an answer not a question?"

"Thugs," says the Wig Man. "They destroyed my shop. Everything is ruined." I never call him back. Instead, my mother buys my sister four wigs made out of strangers' hair. Two brown ones, and two blond. My sister refuses to try the wigs on, so my mother tries them on instead. In the wigs, my mother looks sad and incredibly young. I can see my sister's face gazing out from inside my mother's, like a girl locked inside a tower.

My husband sits on the edge of the bathtub and cries. "We've been here before so many times," he says. "When will it stop?"

"I don't know how much more of this I can take," says the Wig Man.

"Of course my life matters," says Eli. "Why wouldn't it matter?"

"Did you know," says my sister, "that in Disney's *Tangled,* Rapunzel lives inside a kingdom called Corona?"

"That can't be right," I say.

I cut off all my hair. A twelve-inch braid long enough for nobody to climb. I throw the braid into the trash and then remove it from the trash. It's soft and dumb.

"I can't look at it," says my mother.

"Get it away from me," says my sister.

I put it in an envelope and send it to a dear friend's brother, an artist who makes Torahs and animals and money out of human hair and skin. I mean it as an act of solidarity, but I get the feeling my sister and mother read it as an act of pointless sacrifice. To punish Rapunzel for betraying her captivity, the enchantress winds her braids around her left hand, cuts them off, then takes Rapunzel to a wilderness and leaves her there.

"See," I say to my sister. "It's not so bad."

She looks at my short hair, and a small forest grows between us.

Other than Disney's, in no version of Rapunzel is Rapunzel's hair magical. It can't bring back the dead or heal a broken bone or keep a woman young forever. It can't light up dark water. It can't be thrown like a lasso so Rapunzel can glide from mountaintop to mountaintop. It doesn't, like his hair does for Samson, give her a god's power or the strength to kill a lion with her bare hands. It cannot keep a man from being shot for his Blackness. It's just hair.

"I'm sure Rapunzel is wonderful and not terrible," emails a friend, "but also there's something Sisyphean about Rapunzel."

She's right. I know what she means. Rapunzel's hair is no more magical than a mountain the enchantress climbs day after day, pushing the burden of her own spell. I know what she means, but now I am imagining rolling boulders up Rapunzel's back as she bends down to pick the roots and berries she survives on while pregnant in the wilderness. I roll the boulder up Rapunzel's back, and every time I reach the crest, the boulder rolls back down. Rapunzel, the mountain. Rapunzel, my sister.

I am using my sister's cancer to write about the impossible because it's impossible my sister has cancer. And it's impossible my sons cannot go to school or play with their friends. And it's impossible my husband could be shot for being Black. And it's impossible the air is filled with tear gas and viral particles. I have stolen my sister's tiara to wear. I am covered in sweat and dust, and on my head the tiara is crooked. I stole the most beautiful one. I stole the one embellished with glass stones and little pink stars.

It is late afternoon and my sister is sleeping. In the dining room, my mother has lined up all the wigs on their Styrofoam heads. Like four extra daughters. She keeps walking by them and smoothing their hair with her hand. She puts one to her face and inhales. The afternoon light lengthens her shadow. I don't know if she notices I am there.

The story of Rapunzel begins with a pregnant woman's insatiability, her hunger for the finest *rapunzel* (also known as *rampion,* or the "king's cure-all") that results in the barter and entrapment of her daughter. In Giambattista Basile's "Petrosinella," one of the earliest versions of the story, a pregnant woman is caught stealing parsley from an ogress's garden. She apologizes and explains she had to satisfy her craving. In the sixteenth century, there was a widespread belief that if a pregnant woman's cravings weren't satisfied, the shape of whatever she craved would appear on her newborn. Birthmarks are called *voglie* in Italian, which means "longings." My sister and I have identical birthmarks on the right side of our faces. Near our ears. Like a handful of scattered acorns. I am twenty-five years older than my sister. We don't have the same father, but we do have the same mark of our mother's longing.

Every two weeks my mother takes my sister to be infused with poison through a hole in her neck so she doesn't die. My mother looks over at me. I am writing a birthday card with butterflies on it. "I hate butterflies," says my mother. "It's a stupid thing to put on a birthday card. They're barely alive and then they're dead."

Every mother has the exact same single greatest fear. It's the boulder we push while praying for no crest.

"Of course my life matters," says Eli. "Why wouldn't it matter?"

By now the Wig Man must have stopped crying and arrived home. I imagine he is working in the same afternoon light that comes in through my mother's window. He is bent over as he sews each of us, like strands of hair, into a soft net. Listen, we are breathing. You are breathing. My sons and husband are breathing. The Wig Man sews and sews. One piece of glass is still caught in a strand, but he doesn't notice it yet. My mother is breathing. My sister is breathing. We will make a magnificent wig. Rapunzel will wear us in this lost version of her fairy tale. We are not magical, but at least we are alive. "Rapunzel, Rapunzel, / Let your hair down." When she lets us down, what will climb up? We have one last chance to answer right.

21

All the Better to Hear You With

For days Foryst, my cat, seems to have something caught in his throat. I bring him to the vet. "It might be a twig," I say. "Or a pebble."

"What's the cat's name?" she asks.

"Foryst," I say. "Forest," I say again, "but with a *y* where the *e* should go."

The vet is quiet. "How old is Foryst?" she asks.

"Thirteen," I say.

She looks in his mouth.

"It hurts when he swallows," I say.

Foryst is still. The vet sees nothing. She listens to his heart, his lungs. She hears nothing. It suddenly makes no sense to me that she is a human. Why isn't she a wolf with great big eyes and great big ears that are all the better to see him with? To hear him with?

"I recommend blood work," she says.

I put my face in Foryst's fur. "Please tell me what's wrong."

He is silent. There is something in his throat. A word or a dead leaf. I am sure of it.

The vet wants blood work. She wants the cold, definitive clink of numbers. I want Foryst to talk so he can tell me what hurts. I want him to cough up a dry spooked O and be suddenly healed. I want him to tell me the future.

I call my mother. "There's something stuck in Foryst's throat."

"Of course there's something stuck in Foryst's throat," she says. "Why wouldn't there be something stuck in his throat? There's something stuck in all of our throats." She hangs up.

I swallow once. I swallow twice.

When we get home, I open Foryst's mouth and shine a flashlight down his throat. Something shines back, like a diamond in a cave. His teeth are hieroglyphs. I want to jot them down so I can read what's inside him. I want to reach all the way in, but he snaps his mouth shut and growls.

I tell my husband there is something stuck in Foryst's throat.

"What?" he says. He lifts his left headphone from his ear.

"There's something stuck in Foryst's throat."

My husband is always wearing headphones. I say everything twice.

In fairy tales, animals are always talking. Even when they're dead, they're talking.

"Good night, Pinocchio," says the ghost in "The Talking Cricket." "May heaven protect you from morning dew and murderers."

Animals in fairy tales are feral poets. Their words are overgrown and have the scent of soothsayer and pelt. When an animal speaks, it's often to spill the guts of the fairy tale. To leak the plot and indict the antagonist. To clear up the past or tell the future. Animals are tattlers and whistleblowers.

"My mother, she killed me, / My father he ate me," tweets the bird who is the dead boy in "The Juniper Tree."

"Roo, coo, coo, roo, coo, coo / blood's in the shoe / the shoe's too tight, / the real bride's waiting another night," sing the doves in "Cinderella."

"If this your mother knew, / her heart would break in two," moans the horse's head nailed beneath the dark gateway in "The Goose Girl."

First there is an h-u-m. Then there is an h-u-m-a-n. And then there is an a-n. And then there is an a-n-i-m-a-l. Inside fairy tales, *hum* and *human* and *animal* gather like mist. Like humanimals who share a single language.

Outside fairy tales, the mist separates.

The first talking animal, as I was taught by the rabbis, was the snake. "If you eat the apple, your eyes will be opened, and you'll be like God," says the snake, "knowing good from bad." And so Eve ate the apple and knew what God knew.

I ask Eli if he would ever want to know what God knows.

"Of course not," he says. "You would know so much it would be like knowing nothing at all."

The only other animal who talks in the Bible is a donkey who sees an angel in the path of a vineyard. The donkey kneels down, and her master, who does not see the angel, hits her with a stick for kneeling. The master doesn't see the angel because now that we know so much it's like we know nothing at all. Now that we know so much we can barely see the angels.

Foryst surrounds me. He maintains his ability to speak without words. I talk, and I talk, and I talk to him. One of his ears tilts toward me, and the other tilts backward as if catching something the soil just said to the soil.

"Do you think," I ask my husband, "that fairy tales are riddled with talking animals because they're riddled with so little God?"

"What?" he says, lifting his left headphone from his ear.

"Or is there so little God in fairy tales because they're riddled with so many talking animals?"

We bring animals home not only because we are lonely but because we know, as Kafka teaches us, that animals are "the receptacles for the forgotten." Their silence evokes the silence of mourners. Nature, it seems, is trying to forget us. And if we must be forgotten, let us bask in the glow of our animals. Let our fade be warmed by their fur. May the animals beside us keep us upright as we hobble into the future. What has climbed inside

Foryst's mouth might just be something trying to ward off oblivion. It might be something reminiscent of us all.

Kafka called his cough "the animal." His herd of silence. As if Kafka's cough were all of Kafka's stories slowly forgetting Kafka.

Every night I ask my husband, "What's going to happen?"

And every night he says "What," and lifts his left headphone from his ear.

And then I say again, "What's going to happen?" leaving the first "What's going to happen" suspended over our bed.

And my husband says, "With what?"

And every night I say, "With everything."

And every night he says, "I cannot tell you," which sounds like he knows the answer and also sounds like he doesn't know the answer. I wonder if prophets, like animals, must unname the present to see visions of the future.

I'm sorry. I meant to write something happy about what we learn from talking animals in fairy tales, only to realize we learn nothing from them because in fairy tales animals remember everything. And now I've ended up writing about oblivion instead.

"What?" says my husband.

"I've ended up writing about oblivion instead."

Close to my house is a path called Rock and Shoals. It's been raining forever, and I'm worried about what's in Foryst's throat and the end of the world and our democracy and illness and money and hate, and so I decide to take a walk with my sons. The ground is thick with red and yellow and bright-white mushrooms, and the trees are covered in giant snails. One tree seems so swollen, and its bark is shedding such big flakes, that I'm not surprised when a child bursts out. She shakes off the tree from her white hair. She doesn't speak because she is from a future fairy tale where no one speaks, not even the animals.

The girl, my sons, and I walk along the misty path. Her hands are badly rusted and her mouth flickers on and off. *Tell me how this ends,* I want to say, but my words aren't words anymore but limp petals softer than powder.

My sons open their mouths to speak, but where their words should be are pale-green animals with long, spindly newborn legs and round ancient faces. On the ground is a small blue feather, but it isn't small or blue or a feather because this is a fairy tale with no words. I put it in my pocket to bring home, but there is no I or pocket or home because this is a fairy tale with no words. This is a true story, but there is no true or story because this is a fairy tale without words.

When my sons and I without the girl return home, whatever was in Foryst's throat is gone. He is large and soft and his fur is the color of changing leaves. He looks at me and says, *This is how the story*

22

Time to Pay the Piper

It's time to pay the piper. We gather around the old wooden table. No one wants to pay, but it's time. It's one thousand o'clock. Everyone is here. The living and the dead. My grandparents, my mother, my father, my sons, my husband, the rabbis, even the president. You are here, too. Your teachers, your neighbors, your long-lost friends. Everyone you know is here. We put what we can on the table. Everyone must add to the pot. My sons leave wildflower seeds, my husband leaves a rose-colored pendulum, the president mutters and leaves ash, the rabbis leave ink marks scattered like sewing needles, my father leaves his stethoscope. I leave this chapter. I leave my favorite broom. My grandfather leaves a small black key. My grandmother leaves her radiance. My sister leaves her hair.

"I'm not paying," says my mother. "I've paid enough."

The earliest known version of "The Pied Piper of Hamelin" is not a fairy tale but a stained-glass window-pane from a church in Hamelin, Germany, that was destroyed in 1633. Only a shard remains, which Noah pulls from his pocket and holds up to the light. It's the piece of glass with the piper's magical flute. The flute is bronze, and the light catches what's left of the piper's hands. Noah adds the shard to what we'll use to pay the piper.

We miss the old sky. We think if we pay the piper now, the wildfires and the wind and the virus and the floods will swirl back into their wellspring, but the piper is missing. We drag our payment in a large dark sack through the streets calling the piper's name. Our heavy debt. Our hands are blistered and hot, but we must pay the piper. We look for his red-and-yellow-striped scarf and the pipe that hangs from it. We should've paid him long ago, when he emptied our town of rats "who bit the babies in the cradles . . . and made nests inside men's Sunday hats, / And even spoiled the women's chats / By drowning their speaking / With shrieking and squeaking," as Robert Browning wrote. We should have paid him before the sea levels rose and the polar bears thinned. We should have paid him before the first man was shot for the color of his skin, before the first wire was barbed.

But we didn't pay the piper, so the piper made a new song for the children that promised "a joyous land . . . where waters gushed and fruit-trees grew." We didn't pay the piper, and so the children merrily followed him into a mountain, and a disappearing door shut fast when the last child was inside. Now there are no more children.

Now there are no more children, except for one hobbling boy left behind, who couldn't dance into the mountain fast enough. There is always one hobbling boy left behind, to describe the song the children followed. He is the poet. And there is always one rat left behind to describe the song the rats followed. The rat is the poet, too.

On Rosh Hashanah, we blow the shofar one hundred and one times. The blasts alternate between broken howls and long moans. According to the Talmud, the shofar should be a ram's horn because it is hollow and recalls Abraham's near sacrifice of his only son. It recalls Abraham's blind devotion, which blurred only when an angel showed him a ram whose horns were caught in a nearby thicket. Abraham was ready to overpay the piper, but paid with the terrified ram instead.

The shofar we have is broken. My sons take turns blowing it, but all we can hear is silence. It is a beautiful silence. One day when there are too many of me, that is the song I will follow into a mountain. We add the broken shofar to the missing piper's payment.

"Do you ever feel like you're dreaming while you're awake?" asks Eli.

"Sometimes," I say. "Do you?"

"Of course," says Eli. "We are always dreaming. I am a dream and you are a dream and Papa is a dream and

Noah is a dream. Our house is a dream and the earth is a dream."

I add Eli's words to the piper's payment. Into the sack it goes, instantly doubling its worth.

When the piper arrives in Hamelin, he seems to have walked from his "painted tombstone," like an ancestor rising on the "Trump of Doom" (or Judgment Day) to rid the town of a plague. There is, wrote Robert Browning, "no guessing his kith or kin." He is the Godot we barely have to wait for, and then when he arrives, he is the Godot we don't pay. Or is he God, or Guru, or Go? What is his name?

I do not consider myself a follower, even though I have followed things up trees, into rivers, and across bridges. I have listened carefully. I have taken notes and memorized. I have followed instructions, and I have been obsessed. I have been indoctrinated as often as I have pulled up roots and left behind a trail of soil.

Once when I was nine, I was about to follow my father into a mountain when my mother held me back. "Your father," she said, "is brainwashing you."

I had never heard that word before, but it sounded like *bewitched,* and I liked it.

"Look," said my mother. And I looked. My father dipped my brain into a bucket, and sloshed it around in lavender suds. The water was cool and fresh, and it felt like heaven. He folded my brain over a clothesline to dry in the motherless sun. Over my father, I was gaga. Over my mother, I was ungaga.

"See?" said my mother.

I didn't see. Ideology is made out of appetite, and sometimes we are hungry to be famished.

For a long time I followed my father's hum. It never wasn't love. All over my heart are still-glittering flecks from that song I followed. If the piper ever comes to collect payment, I'll put the glittering flecks in the sack, too.

Not once have I seen my son Noah walk in a line with his schoolmates without falling behind or straying, without looking up at the clouds or studying the ants. For better or for worse, I remind myself, he is the poet.

How do we choose what to follow? Or what not to follow? How old is this song we're now following, with its cracked notes and strange ways of stopping and starting? Are we, I wonder, like lemmings to the sea?

"That's a myth," says my husband.

"What is?" I say.

"Lemmings to the sea," he says. "Lemmings don't march blindly to their deaths."

"But it's an idiom," I say. "If it's not like lemmings to the sea, then what is it like?"

"Like humans," says my husband. "Like humans to the sea."

In 1958 Disney made a documentary called *The White Wilderness* to prove that lemmings commit mass suicide by jumping off seaside cliffs. But lemmings don't. The documentary shows hundreds of lemmings jumping into the Arctic Sea, except they're not jumping, and this is not the Arctic Sea. The filmmakers purchased lemmings from children, brought them to the Bow River, and placed them on a turntable to create the effect of a frenzied death march. The lemmings are falling but they do not want to fall. What is happening is not what is actually happening. The film won an Academy Award for Best Documentary.

I wonder what it must feel like to be one of those lemmings. I wonder what it feels like to have been caught and brought to a precipice to perform a myth of yourself. Or maybe that's exactly what we are doing day in and day out. Maybe what we are doing is performing the myth of ourselves on a cliff to the tune of a missing piper's song.

If you see the piper, tell him we have his payment ready. I've added the dreams of a lemming and my favorite orange sweater. This sack is getting heavier and heavier. Tell the piper we don't know how much farther we can carry it while calling for him by a name we've never known. It's now one thousand and one o'clock. It's now later than we ever thought.

23

U Break It We Fix It

I am inside U Break It We Fix It holding my sons' shattered iPad. "Hello," I call out. No one answers. The counter glows white, and the walls are empty. "Hello? Hello?" I wait a few minutes before calling out again.

"One minute," says a raspy voice from the back of the store. Hope swells in my chest. Here We comes. *We will fix it.*

A man in rumpled clothes emerges. I put the shattered iPad on the counter.

"Don't put it there," We says.

I quickly lift it off the counter.

We sprays sanitizer on the spot I touched and wipes it dry with a paper towel.

I hold up the broken screen so We can see It, and a little shard of glass drops to the floor with a plink.

"Yeah, no," We says.

"Yeah no, what?" I ask.

We says the soldering work required would cost more than a new iPad. We says it would take weeks.

"Possibly months." To be sure We asks me to read the serial number off the back of the iPad. I read the numbers, and We silently types them into a computer. "Yeah," We says. "It isn't worth it."

I just stand there. "But if I break It, it says We fix It." I point to the sign that is the name of the store. Even if We has to send it far, far away. Even if it takes the handiwork of one hundred mothers with long white beards and God inside their fingertips, We should fix it. We promised. Even if all We ever do is just *try* to fix It, We should try.

But the man is gone. He has already disappeared into the back of the store.

The next week I return to U Break It We Fix It with a whole entire country. It's heavy, but I manage to carry it through the parking lot, leaving behind a trail of seeds and the crisp scent of democracy and something that smells like blood or dirt. Across it is a growing crack.

A child, too young to be alone, is out in front holding a broken country, too. "Store's gone out of business," says the child. I shift the country to one arm and try to peer in, but it's shuttered and dark. "Told you," says the child. "Out of business."

I text my husband: *"U Break It We Fix It is closed. I've come here for nothing . . . again."*

When I look up, the whole parking lot is full of children holding countries. "Is this U Break It We Fix It?" they ask.

"It once was," says the first child, "but now it's closed."

The children hold their countries closer, like a doll or an animal. I want to drive them all home, but they're all holding countries, and there are far too many of them. "I'm sorry," I say too quietly for any of the children to hear. I don't ask them where their mothers are or how they got here or how they will get home. Instead I walk quickly back to my car.

A little shard of glass falls out of my country with a plink. I pick the shard up and hold it to the sunlight. A rainbow, just for a second, falls over the children. *Plink! Plink! Plink!* Shards of glass are falling out of the children's countries, too. It sounds like an ice storm, but the sky is blue and the children are dry as bones. I don't want to stay to see what happens next. I drive away. I leave the children cradling their broken countries. I have no idea where any of them live, or how to fix anything, or what to do with this shard of glass. At a red light, I put the shard in the glove compartment and forget about it for days.

In Exodus, the first set of ten commandments (broken by Moses) is not buried but placed in the *Aron Hakodesh* (the holy ark) beside the new, unbroken tablets, which the Jews carry through the wilderness for forty years. I imagine the broken tablets leaning against the unbroken ones, telling them secrets only broken things know. I imagine the weight of the broken tablets, and the heat, and the thirst, and the frustration. Why didn't we just leave the broken tablets behind? What good is all this carrying?

To know your history is to carry all your pieces, whole and shattered, through the wilderness. And feel their weight.

"Mama," say my sons one thousand times a day, "can you fix this?" Hulk's head has fallen off, or the knees of a favorite pair of pants are torn, or the bike chain has snapped, or there is slime on Eli's favorite polar bear, or the switch is stuck, or the spring broke off, or Superman's cape is hanging by a thread, or . . .

"What even is this?"

"Oh, that?" says Noah. "It's where the batteries are supposed to go."

"But for what?" I ask.

Noah and I study it for a whole entire minute. "I have zero idea," he says.

What breaks most often in fairy tales are spells, and when a spell is broken, the world is restored. The beast turns back into a prince, the kingdom wakes up, and a girl's tears dissolve the shards of glass in a boy's cold heart. I look up the word *spell*. It means the letters that form a word in correct sequence, and it means a period of time, and it means a state of enchantment. All these things bind. But there is one last definition I catch, at the bottom. *Spell* also means a splinter of wood. What binds is also what cracks off. A spell is also what strays from the whole. This splinter of wood feels like a clue to a mystery I hope to never solve. I add the splinter (that is, a spell) to the shard of glass in my glove compartment. I leave them there together in the dark.

We are knee-deep in broken things. I wade through the kitchen, and the news, and our yard. The dryer is making a sound. The country is divided. Tree limbs are everywhere.

"How did the switch break off the lamp?" I ask Eli.

He shrugs. "It's like a miracle," he says.

In Hans Christian Andersen's "The Snow Queen," a demon makes a mirror in which the image of whatever is good or beautiful dwindles to almost nothing, while the image of anything horrible appears even more horrible: "In the mirror the loveliest landscapes looked like boiled spinach, and the kindest people looked hideous or seemed to be standing on their heads with their stomachs missing." The demon's disciples travel all over the world with the mirror until there is not "a single country or person left to disfigure in it." Then they fly to heaven to distort God and the angels, but the mirror shakes hard with laughter and shatters into a "hundred million billion pieces." The air fills with mirror dust, and the glass blows into the eyes and the hearts of people everywhere. Each shard has the exact same power as the whole entire mirror. Whoever gets mirror in them is cursed with a hardened heart, and with seeing the ugliness of everything.

In Jewish mysticism, there is a phase of Genesis called *Tsim Tsum* that is like the inside-out version of this fairy tale. The glass is not from a demon but from God. According to the cabalists, in order to give the world life, in order to effect creation, God must depart from the world God created. The creator must always exile himself from the creation for the creation to breathe. God contracts to make space so that the world can exist. But right before the departure, God (like a mother) stuffs divine light into vessels that will be left behind. The vessels cannot contain God's light, and burst, scattering shards of light everywhere. Gershom Scholem explained that we spend our lives collecting the offspring of this light. We spend our lives trying to make what once was broken whole again. This, according to the cabalists, begins the history of trauma.

In "The Snow Queen," the good widow crow wraps a bit of black woolen yarn around her leg to grieve her dead sweetheart. I feel I should wrap something around my leg, too. It is almost the middle of November. I grieve for the past four years. They were such sick and tired years, and so much fell to pieces. There is so much mirror dust in our eyes.

"*Move on,*" texts my mother. "*Up and out.*"

I get up and go to my car. I open the glove compartment. The shard is in the shape of a country that seems vaguely familiar, and the splinter is long and sharp like a tongue. I should've stayed with the children and helped them pick up the pieces. Maybe if we had put all our pieces together the pieces would've spelled something. Maybe it would have been a word we need, and now we'll never know.

I drive back to U Break It We Fix It. Someone has painted over the sign, but the words are still legible like a body under a thin sheet. The store is still dark and shuttered, and the parking lot is empty except for a crow who has a bit of black woolen yarn around her leg. The crow stares at me. "Hi, crow," I say.

I notice something shiny in her beak. She drops it at my feet. It's a shard of glass that fits with my shard of glass perfectly. When I put the two pieces together, it looks like a transparent hand reaching out to help someone up. I want to jump for joy. We have only one hundred million billion pieces to go.

In exchange, I give the crow the splinter. She picks it up in her beak where a tongue begins to grow.

Sit down, says the crow. And I sit down in the middle of the parking lot. Just me and the crow on a soft autumn night. *Listen,* says the crow.

And I listen.

24

We Didn't Have a Chance
to Say Goodbye

"I can't find my plague doctor."

"Your what?" says my mother.

"My plague doctor."

"I don't know what that is," says my mother.

I text her a photo of my plague doctor in his ruffled blouse and beak mask sitting on my bookcase a few months before he disappeared.

"I still don't know what that is," says my mother.

"Forget it," I say.

"If you want to find it, then look for it."

"I am looking for it."

"Then look harder."

"I am looking harder."

"It's the strangest thing," I keep saying. But I know it isn't the strangest thing.

I tell everyone who will listen that I've lost my plague doctor. Nine months ago I wrote about seeing the small porcelain doll in a shop in Barcelona and wanting him immediately. If he had been real, his beak mask would've been filled with juniper berries, and rose petals, and mint, and myrrh to keep away a plague I thought belonged only to the past. This was ten years ago. My husband and I were on our honeymoon, and I thought I only wanted the plague doctor. I didn't know I'd eventually need him, too.

"You can't be serious," says my brother. "Who loses a plague doctor during a plague?"

"I guess I do," I say.

"We'll find him," says my husband.

But we never do. The only explanation is that he fell into a donation bag when I was cleaning out closets, and I accidentally dropped him off at Project Safe. "That is not the real name of the thrift store," says my brother. But it really is the real name: Project Safe. I imagine my plague doctor calling for me from the bottom of a bag of old shoes. The news keeps breaking. The number of dead keeps rising. I go on Project Safe's Facebook page. I offer a reward. I will pay whoever bought him five times what they paid. I will donate to the charity of their choice. I will sail across the sea in a paper boat with my pockets full of dried rose petals and fresh air and ancient coins to lure him home.

The manager of Project Safe puts a photo of my plague doctor up by the register. She understands, she tells me, what it feels like to lose something. I feel grateful and ridiculous. The news keeps breaking. The number of dead keeps rising.

I even looked behind the curtains. I even looked in the piano.

The plague doctor is not the only thing I've lost since the pandemic began. The longer I am in my house, it seems, the more things I lose. As if there's a correlation between the hours I inhabit my house and its contents disappearing.

"I could've sworn I put my copy of Virginia Woolf's *The Waves* right here."

"Haven't seen it," says my husband. "I'll help you look."

I look over at our sons. Their rosy cheeks seem to have been replaced by the color of the living room. Is this the year they were supposed to learn all the major rivers? Or is it the year they were supposed to learn how to find the hypotenuse of a triangle?

I could spend months going around this entire house picking up everything that's now lost. I tell my neighbor, the scientist, I've lost my plague doctor. But I don't think he hears me. We're standing too far apart.

My husband leaves the book he is reading, *Journeys Out of the Body,* open on our bed. "That's all we need," I mutter to nobody. I imagine the plague doctor and my husband holding hands on the back of a milk carton. I imagine a toll-free number underneath them in numbers printed so small, it could easily be mistaken for pin-pricks in the carton, the milk leaking out so slowly, it's barely noticeable until it's gone.

I tell our mail carrier I've lost my plague doctor.

"Of course you have, dear," she says. "Everyone

loses their plague doctor." Her hands are small and covered in plastic gloves or fog. She gives me my mail. Nothing is addressed to me.

Sometimes I hear my husband's footsteps coming up the stairs, and I think he's about to knock on my office door with the plague doctor safe in his arms.

What I'm trying to say is that I'm mourning something nameless that has vanished into thin air, and I'm calling it my plague doctor. What I'm trying to say is that we didn't even have a chance to say goodbye. We should've at least had the chance to say goodbye. *Goodbye, plague doctor! Goodbye, old world!* The plague doctor is what I'm holding so I can hold what I'm grieving. Or rather, what I'll never hold again.

I tell Bruno Bettelheim I've lost my plague doctor.

"A child," he says, "needs to understand what is going on within his conscious self so that he can also cope with that which goes on in his unconscious. He can achieve this understanding, and with it the ability to cope, not through rational comprehension of the nature and content of his unconscious but by becoming familiar with it through spinning out daydreams—ruminating, rearranging, and fantasizing about suitable story elements in response to unconscious pressure—"

"Excuse me, Bettelheim, for interrupting you, but what do you think I'm trying to do here?"

Bettelheim looks around. "You lost your plague doctor," he says.

"Vanished into thin air," I say.

A sadness, like a mask, falls over his mouth. His mouth is so beautiful.

"I miss mouths," I say. "I miss my plague doctor. I miss stupidly believing history was lived mostly in the past. I miss not being afraid. . . . Bettelheim?"

"Yes?"

"When will my sons be able to return to their childhoods?"

Bettelheim looks at his wrist where a watch should be. "I could've sworn I was wearing a watch," he says.

The news is breaking. The number of dead keeps rising.

"The child," says Bettelheim, "fits unconscious content into conscious fantasies, which then enable him to deal with that content."

"Like storing my grief inside a figurine?" I ask.

"Yes," says Bettelheim. "It is here that fairy tales have unequaled value because they offer new dimensions to the child's imagination. . . . The form and structure of fairy tales suggest images to the child by which he can structure his daydreams and with them give better direction to his life."

"Which direction are you walking, Bettelheim? I'll walk with you."

We walk slowly down empty street after empty street. He stops at a trash can and looks inside. "You never know," he says.

Other than this fairy tale that is not a fairy tale but

the true story of my missing plague doctor, I can't find a fairy tale in which an object vanishes with no explanation. Even the girl with no hands grows back her hands. Cinderella's glass slipper is never really missing, and when the prince disappears, we know the whole time we can find him inside the beast. Even the darning needle, which breaks and falls down the drain and floats away with the dirty gutter water and is found in the street by schoolboys and is stuck in an eggshell and is run over by a wagon, is never out of our sight. Everything in a fairy tale has already been lost. The fairy tale is where we go to find it again.

I never find my copy of Virginia Woolf's *The Waves*, but if I had, I would've copied this down: "I need silence, and to be alone and to go out, and to save one hour to consider what has happened to my world, what death has done to my world."

I want a lost and found in my living room manned daily by Woolf. A small booth with a sliding window. *Tap tap.* Woolf slides the window open. *State your missing.* And I state my missing. Obviously she never returns anything. But just hearing her sort through the missing is a comfort.

My husband buys me a new plague doctor who is twice the size of my missing plague doctor. Big enough for my missing plague doctor to possibly be hiding inside. Around the new plague doctor's waist is a crescent moon, and from it hangs a lantern, and keys, and an empty birdcage. He is so black and slender and beautiful, he could easily be mistaken for my plague doctor's shadow. He is like the grandmother who comforted me when my grandmother died.

"We wanted to hold," writes the poet Heather McHugh, "what we had."

"I left you a surprise," says Eli. On my desk is a plague doctor made out of clay with a note: "Plage Dok." On its chest is a bright pink heart. Now there are two doctors. One made of shadows, and one made of clay. What we lose is also what we gain. I turn on the faucet and out gush more plage doks. I fill up my glass and I drink and I drink. In the glass, the plage dok's letters rearrange themselves like cells: gold lake, pale opal, old page, aged god. I pull each word from the glass, and carefully dry them before they fade.

"What's that?" asks Eli. "Another story?"

"I hope," I say.

"What's it about?" asks Eli.

"I think it's about saying goodbye."

25

~Hope.docx

I am cleaning my house when I receive a Facebook message from the manager of Project Safe that a volunteer has found my plague doctor, or someone who looks like my plague doctor. The baseboards are thick with dust. I spray a mix of vinegar and lavender and run a rag across them. The plague doctor, or someone who looks like my plague doctor, has been put aside in the office for me. I write back, "Oh! oh! I hope it's him." The rag is black. I am on my hands and knees.

"I hope it's your doll!" writes the manager.

"Fingers crossed," I write back.

It has to be him, I say to no one. *It just has to be.*

I text my mother, *"I'm cleaning the gustroom."* I notice the mistake before I hit send, but I send it anyway. She calls. I pick up.

"I can't move," says my mother. She received her second dose of the vaccine yesterday, and now she's having a reaction.

I tell her the reaction means the vaccine is working.

"I can't lift my arm," she says.

I tell her I've read every version of "Jack and the Beanstalk" I could find because I thought if I followed the hunger and the despair and the cow traded for a pocketful of magic beans and the beanstalk that grows overnight through the clouds and the boy named Jack who climbs the beanstalk and robs a giant of his harp and hen so he and his mother could live happily ever after, I could make a beautiful map of hope because isn't that what we need right now? "Isn't that what we need right now? Hope," I say. "A map of hope."

"Hope?" says my mother, like it's the name of a country she'd never pay money to visit. "What we need is a hell of a lot more than hope."

I tell her the manager of Project Safe just messaged me that a volunteer thinks she might've found my plague doctor, or someone who looks like my plague doctor.

"Here we go again," says my mother, "with the plague doctor." I lost him months ago, and now he's coming home. "Why couldn't she just send you a photo?"

I was wondering that, too, but I don't admit it. If it's not my plague doctor, I want to at least postpone the time in between the darkness and the figure who emerges.

"There's no way it's your plague doctor," says my mother.

"Fee-fi-fo-fum," I say.

"What?" she says.

"I said 'Feel better.'"

In some versions of "Jack and the Beanstalk," every time Jack climbs the beanstalk, his mother grows sicker and sicker. And in other versions, every time Jack climbs back down and shows his mother his gold and tells her he was right about the beans after all, his mother grows quieter and quieter until it's impossible to know if she's even there anymore.

I go to the Centers for Disease Control and Prevention's website. I click on the IF YOU PLANT THEM OVERNIGHT BY MORNING THEY GROW RIGHT UP TO THE SKY link. I want a vaccine, but what I want even more are magic beans I can plant in my arm that will grow into a beanstalk that my sons can climb if they ever run out of hope. I click on the link but it just leads me to a page on "adjusting mitigation strategies." I try to click back, but I can't. My computer freezes. I have to restart.

When my computer turns back on, and I return to this chapter on hope, I realize it wasn't properly saved. Most of it is lost. Only a few old notes, like branches, are scattered across the page. I start to cry and tell my husband I'm giving up writing forever, and then I kick the air, and then I watch tutorials on recovering documents that advise me to search for "hope" with a ~ in front of it. What is that called? A tilde? It looks like a downed beanstalk.

A tilde means "approximately," and it also means an exhausted sigh, like being almost not there, which is the hopeful state I am in when I type the tilde next to *hope*, which is the name of the lost document. In Hebrew, "hope" is *tikvah,* which also means a braided rope or a cord or something you could climb up or climb down, I suppose, like a beanstalk. The tilde could be mistaken for a cutting from a *tikvah,* a cutting I can't imagine being long enough to ever get me anywhere. If I could pinch it off the screen and throw it out the window I would.

Had I turned on Time Machine, I could have recovered my unsaved document, but I didn't even know there was a Time Machine, and so I never turned it on.

In most versions of "Jack and the Beanstalk," at the top of the beanstalk is not the giant's house but dust, a barren desert. There are no trees or plants or living creatures. Famished, Jack sits on a block of stone and thinks about his mother. In Benjamin Tabart's "The History of Jack and the Bean-Stalk," when Jack gets to the top of the stalk, he looks around and finds himself in "a strange country. . . . Here and there were scattered fragments of unhewn stone and at unequal distances small heaps of earth were loosely thrown together." At the highest point of hope is a long empty road. At the top of the beanstalk is dirt that lies fallow so a world can regenerate.

The first known printing of Jack is "The Story of Jack Spriggins and the Enchanted Bean," which is ascribed to a certain Dick Merryman, who wrote he got most of the story from the chitter-chatter of an old nurse and the maggots in a madman's brain. What grows a fairy tale in Merryman's brain is made out of larva and babble, and what's at the top of the beanstalk is a giant named Gogmagog, which sounds like a boy trying to say the word *God* but can't because his mouth is filled with dust.

Project Safe is only a five-minute drive from my house. It's bright and warm and greener than it should be in February. The five-minute drive feels too short. Shouldn't my hope and the fulfillment of my hope be farther apart? Shouldn't it take my whole life to drive to Project Safe?

My heart is beating fast. I park and go inside. I go past the racks of donated clothes, and coffee mugs, and old couches, and books. My heart is beating faster. I can already feel the weight of my plague doctor's small porcelain body in my hand, his soft velvet coat. I want to call out *I'm here!* because I'm once again close enough to the plague doctor for him to hear me. *I've come at last!* I want to sing.

And then I see her. I see the volunteer who found my plague doctor or someone who looks like my plague doctor. She knows it's me. She looks like my stepdaughter. She knows I've come to retrieve what I've lost. "It's in here," she says brightly.

I follow her. She smells like oranges, and her smile is so beautiful. She leads me to a back office filled with bags and bags of donations. "Wait here," she says.

I wait and in my waiting I know something is wrong. She returns too quickly. There is too little dust. What she is holding is not my plague doctor. It's a mask of a plague doctor, and this mask is the size of my face. I don't know if it is wooden or plastic because I back away from it immediately and say something like no or "thank you for trying" or "he is much smaller and he has arms and legs." I wave goodbye to the volunteer as if I am in the ocean and she is on the shore instead of where we really are, which is standing barely ten feet apart in the back room of a thrift store.

On my way out the door, I stop because I notice a small rusted harp leaning against a ceramic brown hen with a crack running along one wing.

I bring both to the register. "Just these two?" asks the volunteer.

"Yes," I say. "Just these two."

I smile so I do not cry. "Thank you again for trying," I say.

I leave my car in the Project Safe parking lot and climb down the beanstalk with the hen and the harp in the pocket of my coat. My mother is waiting for me at the bottom. She is no longer feverish, and she shows me she can now lift her arm. I would give her the hen and the harp, but when I reach into my pocket, I realize both have turned to dust. Now my hands are covered with dust, and as the dust falls from my hands, it looks like the ellipses to all the stories we thought were over but are still being told. My sons come outside and ask for some dust. I give them each a handful because there is so much dust. They sprinkle it all over our yard, and their sprinkling looks like ellipses, too.

"Did you know," says Noah, "that without dust there would be no clouds?"

"No," I say, "I didn't know that."

"It's true," says Eli. "There'd be no clouds if we had no dust."

My mother, my sons, and I all look up at the sky. It's so blue and there are so many clouds.

"That one's shaped like a giant," says Noah.

"And that one, Mama, is shaped like your mouth," says Eli.

And one cloud, the one hardest to see but I promise it's there, is shaped exactly like what you'd always hoped it to be.

26

Ever After

"Mama," says Eli, "there are two Mavises."

I look in Mavis's cage, and sure enough there are two of her. After a long summer in New York visiting my mother, my sons and I arrive home to find Eve's tarantula has molted. The skin she crawled out of looks no different from what she has become.

Eli touches Noah's arm. "Look," he says, "there are two Mavises."

Noah looks through the glass. "If there are two Mavises, how do we know which one is Mavis?"

"I think," says Eli, "they both are."

We haven't seen Eve for almost two years. When she left to go live with her mother, she left Mavis behind. The crickets she eats are seventeen cents each. The salesperson hands me an inflated plastic bag with a dozen crickets. I drive home with them on the passenger seat. They chirp and cling to the sides of the bag, and I try not to look. Buying live crickets has become the last shred of my stepmothering.

When I get home, I hand the bag to my husband so he can feed Mavis.

"You bought medium crickets. She eats large."

"She'll live," I say.

And she does. Mavis lives.

For the first few days after molting, Mavis is so vulnerable, even a small brush-up against Old Mavis could badly wound her. I unzip the bursting suitcases and begin unpacking. We were at my mother's for far too long. We overstayed our welcome. What I thought was still home has moved on, and what I thought had moved on inside me still has a long way to go. I missed my husband. I missed Georgia and how it wears its ghosts on the outside like peeling paint. I missed being a mother at a distance from my mother. After weeks against the backdrop of my childhood, my sons are relieved to be back inside their own. I think I will go nowhere now for a long, long time.

I've never seen Mavis move. Not even once. She reminds me of all the letters of all the alphabets neatly piled on top of one another. Though I've never seen it happen, occasionally an untucked serif must tremble. The tinged stem of her aleph, without sun, must eventually wilt. Mavis's belly is the unutterable center of every tale. Look how far she has gone by staying perfectly still.

"I have done nothing all summer," wrote Georgia O'Keeffe, "but wait for myself to be myself again."

In fairy tales, a child who is born as a sprig of myrtle, or an apple, or half a hedgehog will eventually burst from that shape into a more human one. A kiss can disenchant a swallow and turn it back into a boy. Fury turns princes into frogs and princesses into silence, and treading on a mother's heart can turn a child into stone. In fairy tales, forms can unbutton like overcoats, drop to the ground, and vanish without a trace. My body has softened and thickened. I am more pond than tree. More cloud than seed. If I unbuttoned now, what would be underneath? Stories, like broken water? A regret, like a wild vine blanketed in snow? A joke so wrinkled, it's begun to resemble a poem? How many overcoats have I shed, and how will I know when I've reached my last layer?

"I'm so happy to be home," I say to my husband. I fall into his chest, breathe in his earth, and stay there for one thousand years.

A hard, stiff piece of me cracks off my shoulder. My husband picks it up. It fits perfectly in his palm, like a crust of bread. It's as colorless as the youngest hour. What is underneath is an idea I won't have for a long time.

My sister's treatment is over. Her hair is slowly growing back. What once was long and golden is now a shock of red. She wants to move to California and become a star. She sends me a link to her YouTube makeovers. She is a swan, she is a mermaid, she is a sorceress, she is Medusa, she is a skull, she is Rapunzel. She goes step by step. She guides her followers so they, too, can get the exact same look.

A few days after we return home, I check on Mavis. Her old skin is gone. "Did she eat it?" I ask my husband.

"No, no," he says. "I threw it in the trash."

Now there is only one Mavis.

Sasha's transformations are as spellbinding as Mavis's. The fading scar on her neck where the chemo port once was is the length and width of one of Mavis's legs. No, it's smaller. Like a stray thread that can't be brushed away.

Is the fairy tale the very last skin a story sheds, or is the fairy tale its first? Maybe it's both, which could explain why the fairy tale keeps not dying.

The fairy tale is a fossil you can plant like a seed.

I open Genesis, and a slip of paper falls out. The handwriting is mine but younger: "And God said, let there be a fairy tale and there was a fairy tale. And God saw the fairy tale, and it was good."

I flip through the pages looking for more, but nothing. Just a dried oak leaf bookmarking where Lot's wife turns into a pillar of salt because she looked, just for a split second, behind her.

Sometimes a spider gets stuck inside its old carapace. Most of the time it's just a small part of the body, but if the spider becomes trapped inside her old skin for too long, she could die. I pour a cup of apple juice for Eli and ask him what he thinks the hardest part of being human is. It's been a long day, and the afternoon light sleepily stretches over his soft dark curls.

"I think the hardest part of being human," says Eli, "is trying to forget what you don't want to remember."

I want to ask him what he's trying to forget, but I know not to.

My mother calls. "I figured out the problem," she says.

At first I think she means the problem with me or the choices I've made, or with her, or with our long summer, or with mothers in general, or with fairy tales, or with children, or with freedom, or with cancer, or with money, or with the future, or with love, or with the planet, or with the past, or with my father, or with Georgia, or with religion, or with New York, or with aging, or with just being alive.

"It wasn't the bed," says my mother. "It was the bed-sheets. I need a larger thread count. Otherwise it's impossible to sleep."

"How many threads do you need?"

"One thousand," she says, "at the very least."

There is a Jewish myth that in the womb, an angel lights a candle allowing us to see from one end of the earth to the other, and then right before we are born the angel taps us between our nose and our mouth, leaving a dent, so that we forget everything. But as we grow, change shape, come loose, and rebuild, what we forget still guides us.

If a fairy tale had a shape, it would be this dent. If a mother had a shape, it would be this dent. If my love for this terrible, beautiful world had a shape, it would be this dent. If I could choose my final form, it would be this dent, between Noah's and Eli's mouth and nose. If I could choose my final form, I would want it to be where my sons must forget everything in order to remember.

Until then, I will walk this dent like a path through the woods.

I check on Mavis. Her new skin now has the slightest tint of midnight blue. It must be the same blue that's inside the angel's flame.

An Epilogue: After Ever

First it was basic multiplication, then decimals using grids, then variable expressions and coordinate planes. Then it was identifying three-dimensional figures viewed from different perspectives. By October, Noah asked if I could help him count vertices, edges, and faces. He had already found the volume of rectangular prisms. He had solved a whole page of multistep word problems involving remainders, then asked me to check it, but how?

I stared at his homework. There were missing operators. There were stem and leaf plots to interpret. Occasionally there were tears in the page from too much erasing. Holes where numbers should go. Each day the problems got harder. Each day there were more of them to solve.

"Dear Mrs. Bloom," I wrote, "in problem #18 there seemed to be no missing number yet Noah was asked to find it."

"Dear Mrs. Bloom, there were more problems than Noah could solve in a single night. He did his best."

"Dear Mrs. Bloom, Noah did all his homework then crumpled it up in despair. I smoothed it out as best I could."

By winter, the problems Noah brought home left us both in tears. "What even is this?" I asked my husband. Neither of us knew. I turned the page upside down. "If you hold it like this, it reminds me of that mythical sea creature with the tentacles. What is it called?"

"Kraken?" said my husband.

"Yes," I said. "Kraken."

A *P* on Noah's report card meant "progressing," which is what Noah received. He was striving for an *M*, which meant "meet." He hadn't yet met what he was meant to meet, but Mrs. Bloom wrote, in cheerful cursive, that she knew he was well on his way to meeting it.

By late winter, the math seems to soften. Whereas before he was asked to evaluate numerical expressions with parentheses in different places, now he is just being asked to add. The numbers are large, practically swollen, but adding them is so much easier than what he had been asked to solve in the fall.

"Dear Mrs. Bloom, is this Noah's math homework? It seems much less challenging than before."

"Dear Mrs. Bloom, Noah tells me all the children are now just adding whole numbers, is this correct or is it only Noah?"

"Dear Mrs. Bloom, can you tell me the pedagogical reasons for returning to the beginning?"

Two days after Noah's only homework is to subtract

1000 from 1000, he comes home with just the number 1. It is large enough to fill the entire page. A blade of grass. Noah colors it green.

Outside, it is mistier than usual. A castle rises in the distance.

"Is that a castle?" I ask my husband.

"Sure looks like it," he says.

A light from the tower flickers on once, then twice. A large crow lands in our yard. The neighbors stand on their porches, worried. "What do you think is going on?" one calls to the other. There is nothing about any of this on the news. The news is fading.

"Did you know," says Eli, "the first evidence of the existence of the number one was a series of unified lines cut into bone?"

"It was a baboon's bone," adds Noah.

"Its fibula," says Eli.

"Twenty thousand years ago in the Congo, someone was trying to keep track of something, but of what?" says Noah.

"Maybe miracles or food," says Eli.

"How do you know all this?" I ask. They sound like their tongues are wrapped in old wool.

"That's what the children are learning now," says Noah. Just *1*. "I told you. It wasn't just me. You always think it's just me, but it's all of us."

"It's all of us," says Eli. "Mama, "it's time for us to return to the beginning." His eyes twinkle like the eyes of a hundred-year-old man.

I call my mother. I tell her about the 1. How green it is now. How sometimes it even seems to sway. I tell her what Eli and Noah told me about the marks on the bone, and I tell her about the castle, too.

"What?" says my mother. "I can't hear you."

"What's that in the background?" I ask.

"Wolves," she says.

At night, I wake up to get a glass of water, and the 1 is humming. It glistens on the kitchen counter. I put it in the belt of my robe like a sword. I stand on the porch.

Noah is up, too. He heard a sound, he said. Galloping. "And when I looked out my bedroom window," he says, "I saw a white horse staring up at me wearing a necklace of pink roses."

I follow him to his bedroom and look out the window. "Go back to sleep," I say. "It's okay. Nothing is there."

"Why are you wearing the 1?" asks Noah.

"I don't know," I say. "It was humming."

"Oh, I know," says Noah. "It does that sometimes."

I look out the window again. Our car is gone. I wake my husband up. "The car is gone. Come look." He is flatter than I remember him. His beard, longer. He gets up and walks to the porch. "See?" I say. "The car is gone."

My husband lights his pipe. "The world's a new color," says my husband. "And where are the brothers?"

"They're upstairs sleeping. . . . Noah woke up. . . . He said he saw a white horse wearing a necklace of pink roses."

My husband takes a puff of his pipe, and the smoke makes the shape of our sons holding hands.

About a week before the *1*, I had hired a man to install a window in my office. I would be able to watch the sun slowly rise as I wrote. I would be able to see the sky. The man even promised me a ledge where I could put a small plant. A fern, I imagined. But when the man cut a hole in the wall, it became obvious that in order for there to be any view at all, he'd also have to build a tunnel on account of our slanted roof, and on account of where the wall was, and there was another reason I cannot remember. "The effect," he said, as he sketched something, then erased something, then measured the wall again, "would be like looking through a telescope."

"That doesn't sound good," I said.

"I'm sorry," he said.

I looked at the hole in my wall. It reminded me of Noah's math homework where he erased too hard. The insides of my house were showing.

"I will patch it up," he said. "It will be like none of this ever happened."

I hold the *1* up to where the window couldn't be, and the *1* glows. "Did you see that?" I say. But there's no one standing beside me to answer.

I go downstairs and open the front door. It's all woods. "Hello," I call out.

A king walks sadly by dragging his velvet robes. The fog is thick. A boy flies over the trees. Whatever paint this town in Georgia was once covered in has been stripped away. The white horse with the necklace of pink roses steps out of the thick mist, shakes flakes of paint from its mane, and nuzzles the *1*.

"Doesn't it feel like we're becoming nobody and everybody," asks Eli, "at the same time?"

"It does," I say.

"It does," says Noah, who is now holding the *1*.

The *1* is beginning to look less and less like the marks on a twenty-thousand-year-old bone, and more like the bone itself.

"Don't let the horse eat it," I say.

"I would never dream of eating it," says the horse. "It's for all of us," says the horse.

My husband joins us. He lights his pipe. "The world's a new color. And where are the brothers?"

"We are right here, Papa," says Noah.

"We are right here, Papa," says Eli.

My husband takes a puff from his pipe. The smoke spells every word of this fairy tale.

"How did you do that, Papa?" "Can I try?" "Can I?"

I call my mother. "It feels like the world is bursting out of its skin."

"Here we go again," says my mother. I hear a soft howl.

"Wolves?" I say.

"No," she says. But I know the wolves are there. "What grade did Noah get in math?" asks my mother.

"*P*," I say. "For 'progressing.' "

"All this weighs heavily on my heart," says my mother.

"You don't sound like my mother," I say.

"Well you don't sound like my daughter," says my mother.

"How are you calling me," I ask, "inside a fairy tale?"

"How are you answering?" she asks.

The *1* grows so big, my husband and sons and I carry it through the woods to a glittering lake. We slide it into the water like a raft and climb on. The horse and my mother and the wolves and the neighbors and Mrs. Bloom and the man who cut a hole in my wall then patched the hole up and the sad king and the flying boy and the baboon and the crow climb on, too. There is room for all of us. There is even room for you. The *1* grows bigger and lowers as the lake rises. The lake is now just a drop of water at the center of the *1*. And we are specks. Pencil marks on paper. Waiting to be solved.

Acknowledgments

To Nadja Spiegelman, the fairy godmother of this book, without whom there would be no *Happily*. To *The Paris Review* for giving *Happily* a place to grow. To Mark Warren, Robin Desser, Parisa Ebrahimi, and to the whole Random House team for clearing the path so I could find my way home. To Sarah Bowlin, guiding light.

Had Danielle Dutton and Martin Riker not saved my stories at the eleventh hour, I don't know where I'd be. Definitely not here.

To the Creative Capital Foundation, thank you.

To Kristen Iskandrian, for your gigantic friendship, which is also a miracle.

To Amy Margolis, for holding my hand through the scary woods and cracking me up along the way.

To the Athens-Clarke County Library for the writing desk under the painting of the snowstorm.

To all my students, past, present, and future.

To my dear friends and family (near and far) who

inspire me daily, especially: Samara Scheckler, Hope Hilton, Sarah Baugh, Amy Bramblett, Ed Pavlic, Stacey Barnum, Mary Katherine Dunwoody, the Wislars, the McMakens, Daniel Khalastchi, Will Walton, Tyler Goodson, Deirdre Sugiuchi, Amber Dermont, Robyn Schiff, Katiedid Langrock, Mika Hadani, Jane Elias, John Woods, Brian Connell, Larry Walton, Danielle Mark, Brielle Mark, Ronnie Gorden, Sasha Worenklein, Jay Worenklein, Harriet Bass, and Eve McKnight.

To the many writers and artists whose work lights up this terrible, beautiful world, especially Margaux Kent, Ariel Burger, Ilya Kaminsky, Katie Farris, Kate Zambreno, Elizabeth McCracken, Edward Carey, Aimee Bender, Maria Dondero, Lamar Peterson, and Christina Forrer.

To Bruno Schulz and Leonora Carrington, I know you don't know me, but you found me when I was very lost.

In memory of my grandparents, especially Gertrude Mark, whom I miss every day.

To my mother, for keeping me real.

To my father, for keeping me unreal.

To Ari Mark, for believing in my wishes before I even blow the candle out.

To Etan Mark, the truest bluest of them all.

To Reg, dearest mystic. For the spells and this life. You are my home, my ever after.

This book is for Noah and Eli. I love you.

ABOUT THE AUTHOR

Sabrina Orah Mark is the author most recently of *Wild Milk,* a collection of fiction, as well as the poetry collections *The Babies* and *Tsim Tsum.* She lives in Athens, Georgia, with her husband and two sons.

ABOUT THE TYPE

This book was set in Sabon, a typeface designed by the well-known German typographer Jan Tschichold (1902–74). Sabon's design is based upon the original letter forms of sixteenth-century French type designer Claude Garamond and was created specifically to be used for three sources: foundry type for hand composition, Linotype, and Monotype. Tschichold named his typeface for the famous Frankfurt typefounder Jacques Sabon (c. 1520–80).